SELECTED POEMS
1955-1980

IAIN CRICHTON SMITH

Selected Poems
1955 - 1980

SELECTED BY

ROBIN FULTON

MACDONALD PUBLISHERS
Loanhead, Midlothian

ISBN 0 904265 55 2

Published by
Macdonald Publishers
Edgefield Road, Loanhead, Midlothian

*The publisher acknowledges the financial
assistance of the Scottish Arts Council
in the publication of this volume*

Printed in Scotland by
Macdonald Printers (Edinburgh) Limited
Edgefield Road, Loanhead, Midlothian

PREFACE

IAIN CRICHTON SMITH's first *Selected Poems* was published by Gollancz in 1970. This drew on his first five collections: *The Long River* (Macdonald, 1955); *The White Noon* (1959), *Thistles and Roses* (1961) and *The Law and the Grace* (1965), all three published by Eyre & Spottiswoode; and *From Bourgeois Land* (Gollancz, 1969). It also included work at that time not collected in book form, such as poems from the Iain Crichton Smith issue of *Lines Review* (No. 29, 1969). The selection in Penguin Modern Poets 21 (1972) almost entirely duplicated material from the 1970 selection.

Books go out of print: prolific writers go on being prolific. *Love Poems and Elegies* (1972), *The Notebooks of Robinson Crusoe* (1975) and *In the Middle* (1977) were published by Gollancz. *Orpheus and Other Poems* (1974) was published by Akros. And *Hamlet in Autumn* (1972) and *The Permanent Island* (1975) were published by Macdonald in the Lines Review Editions Series. By 1980 there had also been several pamphlets and a wide scattering of uncollected items in various magazines.

The time seemed right for a new *Selected Poems* and I was asked to make the selection. The choice of poems and their arrangement are therefore mine. Other editors would of course have chosen this or that differently but I hope I have included most of the work that most readers most admire. Naturally, the book was compiled with the co-operation of Iain Crichton Smith and with his approval of the final arrangement.

The main sources of each section are as follows:

I: *Lines Review* Nos. 6, 16, 21, 22, 24; *New Poems* 1959; *Thistles and Roses*.

II: *The Law and the Grace*; *Deer on the High Hills* (published separately by Giles Gordon in 1962).

III: *The Permanent Island*, Part One, translated by the author from *Biobuill is Sanasan Reice* (1965).

IV: *Lines Review* No. 29; *From Bourgeois Land*; *Three Regional Voices* (Poet and Printer, 1968).

V: *Lines Review* Nos. 26, 29; *Scottish Poetry Three* (Edinburgh University Press, 1968); *Scottish International Review* (August, 1969); *The Permanent Island*, Part Two, translated by the author from *Eadar Fealla-dha is Glaschu* (1974).

VI: *Lines Review* Nos. 29, 51; *Hamlet in Autumn*.

VII: *Hamlet in Autumn*; *Lines Review* Nos. 51, 54.

VIII: *Love Poems and Elegies*; *Poems for Donalda* (Ulsterman, 1974).

IX: *Orpheus and Other Poems*; *The Notebooks of Robinson Crusoe*.

X: *In the Middle*; and uncollected poems first published in *Chapman, Lines Review, The Scotsman, Scrivener, Stand* and the *TLS*.

Acknowledgements are due to all the publishers and magazines mentioned.

ROBIN FULTON

CONTENTS

I

III

IV

VII

VIII

IX

X

I

POEM OF LEWIS

Here they have no time for the fine graces
of poetry, unless it freely grows
in deep compulsion, like water in the well,
woven into the texture of the soil
in a strong pattern. They have no rhymes
to tailor the material of thought
and snap the thread quickly on the tooth.
One would have thought that this black north
was used to lightning, crossing the sky like fish
swift in their element. One would have thought
the barren rock would give a value to
the bursting flower. The two extremes,
mourning and gaiety, meet like north and south
in the one breast, milked by knuckled time,
till dryness spreads across each ageing bone.
They have no place for the fine graces
of poetry. The great forgiving spirit of the word
fanning its rainbow wing, like a shot bird
falls from the windy sky. The sea heaves
in visionless anger over the cramped graves
and the early daffodil, purer than a soul,
is gathered into the terrible mouth of the gale.

THE GOOD PLACE

You'd say it was a good place if you knew it,
the adults friendly and the children happy.
A landscape for a certain kind of poet
who wrote in miniature and at times was sloppy.

Who saw umbrellas mushroom through the winter,
was dazzled by oceans on a summer day,
made tactful noises at the local painter,
saw cardboard yachts heel stiffly round the bay.

Heard Sundays punished by the fighting bells:
attended lectures: strolled by the salt shore:
imagined bees content with honeyed cells:
listened with patience to a crashing bore.

You'd say it was a good place except that sometimes
a wish for terror and for lightning strode
down the great mountains to the village rhymes
to find in lakes the wicked face of God.

FOR MY MOTHER

You have so little and that I have more
(money, I mean) angers me. As well,
I had four years at University where
I sipped good learning under a proud bell.

You on the other hand were gutting herring
(at seventeen) on a hard Lowestoft quay
with glassy hands to which dark blood would cling
while the red clouds would lighten on the sea.

Angrily I watch you from my guilt
and sometimes think: The herring in my hand,
bloody and gutted, would be far more solid
than this more slippery verse, but that cold wind

appals me as a voluntary price to pay,
the lonely figure in the doubtful light
with the bloody knife beside the murmuring sea
waiting for the morning to come right.

4

THE PLACE

To reach the place where there is no enigma
and there to exist quietly like a horse
or a cat daintily licking its paws
by a green lane among cool shadows.

I speak now as if I wasn't here.
Nothing comes between me and my speech
except the necessary oxygen
and the landscapes that I endlessly leaf through.

What fidgetings there were once.
How in sour railway stations I sought God
thinking I would take a train to somewhere
distant, remarkable and full of lights.

Perhaps the enigma's breaking like a boil
leaving the head as it was, an object
turning at random on a narrow stalk
towards the white sun that is always there.

ABERDEEN

Mica glittered from the white stone.
Town of the pure crystal,
I learnt Latin in your sparkling cage,
I loved your brilliant streets.

Places that have been good to us we love.
The rest we are resigned to.
The fishermen hung shining in their yellow
among university bells.

Green laws and clinging ivy. Mediaeval
your comfortable lectures, your calm grammar.
The plate glass windows showed their necklaces
like writhing North Sea fish.

Nothing will die, even the lies we learn!
Union Street was an arrow
debouching on the crooked lanes, where women
sweated like leaking walls.

SCHOOL TEACHER

She was always earlier than the bell at nine.
She trod the same stone street for forty years.
(The stone might show a broken-backed design
of prints that slowly slant from toe to heel
as the years told). Boy saluted well
as, morning-mounted, light struck spinning wheels
of cycles heading schoolward. Poets' lines
shimmered within boys' cheering. Globes and faces
spun, blurred. Open atlases
shouted their naked countries, bright as paint
created for her pupils. ('Stand. Recite.')
And who stood up? John's father? John? The faint
graph of her will climbed the wavering wall.
It climbed for forty years. It made a white
snake on distemper. ('Who was the famous saint
who crossed from Ireland in a flimsy boat,
Columba or Columbus? Surely you remember?'

'Remember, answering questions you must quote.
Never forget what the poet really wrote.')

The iambic's broken by the clanging bell.
The room's destroyed by noise, by leaving feet.
What was the message she had tried to tell
for forty years? She knew she had a debt
to pay for living. It had started well.
Yes, there was something she had tried to tell.
She'd never told it, for the moment passed
into the seething waters as a cast
wavers in underwater, taking shape
from shaken river movement, from the swell.
Yes, there was something. But she could not tell.
The walls wavered into moving lines.
John? John's father? stood in a bright class
hurrying the dead metres of his race
well-brushed, well-mannered. Irony perhaps?
Was that the message—that we'll never learn?
That all our atlases having shining maps?

The classroom wavered. The four walls poured in.
Her barren gown hung in the sea's spin.
'I want that apple. Bring it here at once.'
And smilingly he came to lay it flat

on the clear desk. It hissed like a red cat:
and standing quietly by her unlearnèd breast
the boy's eyes shone with an oblique unrest.
Sighing, she locked the lid. The apple lay
placed in her loved desk, soon to decay.

THE WIDOW

That's his harem on the shelves.

                           I don't know
whether to keep them or to ask some men
to take and marry them. Would that be wrong,
a posthumous divorce? No, I think no,
they shall bed here: at least they'll have a roof
even though he's gone without a single proof
of late repentance. But—'he had a stroke'—
how could he show repentance? Being aloof
was always his best nature. I had proof.
Surely if anyone knows I ought to know.
Let me be clear—his chair is rocking now
as if he's sitting in it writing scripts
for his societies—(Lamb it was he liked
of all the writers—he had wounded wings).

He should have told me forty years ago.
The church echoed my wifehood. There is no
happiness like that, the golden rings
growing to children's curls. And then the snarl,
barren and savage, on our wedding night.
The light burned late, the bare electric light
mocked my new body: You're an ageing girl.
The two rooms shook loudly in the night.
It wasn't right. No, though you're sitting there
it wasn't right, I tell you. You were tired
or so you told me when you came from where
you taught your pupils. They at least were fired
by passions that your bookishness could share
only by proxy. You would make them write
their growing into grammar ('would' to 'might').
And then you were a child again. The stroke
twitched your left eye. I towered you lying white
each gaping morning. What it was that broke

was mended out of pity by the night.
I did not love you. I did what I would do
for any sufferer. You had gone beyond
the limits of the landscape that I knew.
I'll not be jealous of books. I can't afford
to let this anger shake me. The white sword
rusts in the bookcase. It's a thousand years
since I first met you. 'Clever lad' they said
'and diligent as well, but, more than these
a faithful son, his mother's tireless nurse.'
O, it's what I knew. Your bedroom's polished board
shakes with your pacing. It was you, not me,
whose anguish throbbed the house when like a tree
you felt your birds all leave you, without a word
hunched at your glittering window. What went free
that should have stayed? Your heart clicked like a glove.
Perhaps you loved me as you loved those boys
and girls you taught, leading to stricter joys
their halting minds? Perhaps it was love
the spirit not the flesh might understand.
Why did you marry me? (I long to know.)
I hear you saying: 'They must learn to love
the purest light shed from the purest mind'
as, raincoated and thin, you'd strike through wind
into the endless struggle to be true
to what is most untrue, the being-bound
to loveless loving. Should I read your books
not leave them in the glass case where I found
them, neatly ordered? You can write each night
here on this table. I will rub it white.

How could you forgive me if you could
never forgive yourself? That's why you're dead.
'There's nothing to forgive,' I might have said
but that's untrue. You know it is untrue.
Could you expect from me a gratitude
I could not feel? Often in the night
I heard you tossing like a guilty child
calling his mother through the shaken wood.
You wouldn't marry till she died. I knew
or thought I knew that that was true and right.
Can I forgive you or be reconciled
when you would scourge yourself? It's past my knowing.
Are there such people whose true life is dying?

8

O, if there are, you certainly were one
Whose best success was failure.
                              To cease growing—
that is the worst of all. Therefore must I
hug your cold shoulders all the wintry night
and summer too? Old woman like a sky
open to rain and lightning. Am I God
so to forgive you or to leave the Why
nailed to my cross? Your chair is rocking, rocking,
as if with grief. I see you with a rod
whipping your bony body. Stop, I say.
Stop, child, you mustn't. You were all I had.

STATEMENT BY A RESPONSIBLE SPINSTER

It was my own kindness brought me here
to an eventless room, bare of ornament.
This is the threshold charity carried me over.
I live here slowly in a permanent

but clement weather. It will do for ever.
A barren bulb creates my firmament.
A sister cries: 'I might have learned to wear
sardonic jewellery and the lineament

of a fine beauty, fateful and austere.
I might have trained my perilous armament
on the learned and ferocious. A lover
would have emerged uniquely from that element.'

I know that for a lie, product of fever.
This is my beginning. Justice meant
that a man or woman who succumbs to fear
should not be married to good merriment.

I inspect justice through a queer air.
Indeed he lacks significant ornament.
Nevertheless he does not laugh or suffer
though, like pity's cruelty, he too is permanent.

And since I was trapped by pity and the clever
duplicities of age, my last emolument
returns, thus late, its flat incurious stare
on my ambiguous love, my only monument.

9

IN LUSS CHURCHYARD

Light strikes the stone bible like a gong:
blank leaves gape open. Greenness of grass is most
what, raging round the slabs, astonishes
the casual visitor drifting like a ghost
among the inscriptions and the wishes
chiselled on stone, prayed for a dead tongue.

A bird flickers from bough to windless bough
unsettled, frenzied perhaps with heat
or violence of the breast, a pagan joy.
The stranger remarks anew his moving feet
so constantly labouring in his employ
and walking without thought as they do now:

and the very inscriptions mirror modes of death—
the early stately and the later terse
(the very early almost invisible).
Consider how this eighteenth-century verse
glides with a quiet charm through pastoral
landscapes of the wandering breath.

Here however a skull, there crossed bones
leap out with tigerish instancy, like fire
burning through paper: with a savage force
punch through electric noon where the hands perspire
and prickle with the sun. This is indeed a coarse
imagery to be carved on harmless stones.

The adjacent river rambles quietly on
with wayward music, hardly disturbing even
the image of a leaf or stone or stick
but holding all the amplitude of heaven—
the fiery blueness of a composed Atlantic—
arching an earth poised in the breathless noon

where living and dead turn on the one hinge
of a noon intensely white, intensely clear.
The eyes read dates: the hands steady and rest
on leaning stone without a twitch of fear
merely an aimless curiosity. The breast,
empty with indifference, broods in change.

Yet, should a charge populous, terrible,
burst through the feeding greenness, capsizing this
mound like a knotted table, knees would sink
into the imponderable abyss
where the one star burns with a convulsive wink
in a white sky, blown outwards like a bubble.

The silence holds. A saw nags at a tree.
The settled bird chirps briefly while a breeze
ruffles its breast. The eye confused by dates
is pleasurably excited by the trees
arching a coolness over the heavy gates.
Therefore out of the noon's implacable sea

of hammered light the feet, still steady, go.
The hands touch wood and push the gate away
from the dreaming body which casts a little shade.
Out of the hectic greenness into a day
of dusty roadways the feet, suddenly gripping, wade
gathering power, changing to swift from slow.

LUSS VILLAGE

Such walls, like honey, and the old are happy
in morphean air like gold-fish in a bowl.
Ripe roses trail their margins down a sleepy
mediaeval treatise on the slumbering soul.

And even the water, fabulously silent,
has no salt tales to tell us, nor makes jokes
about the yokel mountains, huge and patient,
that will not court her but read shadowy books.

A world so long departed! In the churchyard
the tilted tombs still gossip, and the leaves
of stony testaments are read by Richard,
Jean and Carol, pert among the sheaves

of unscythed shadows, while the noon day hums
with bees and water and the ghosts of psalms.

11

FOR THE UNKNOWN SEAMEN OF
THE 1939-45 WAR
BURIED IN IONA CHURCHYARD

One would like to be able to write something for them
not for the sake of the writing but because
a man should be named in dying as well as living,
in drowning as well as on death-bed, and because
the brain being brain must try to establish laws.

Yet these events are not amenable
to any discipline that we can impose
and are not in the end even imaginable.
What happened was simply this, bad luck for those
who have lain here twelve years in a changing pose.

These things happen and there's no explaining
and to call them 'chosen' might abuse a word.
It is better also not to assume a mourning,
moaning stance. These may have well concurred
in whatever suddenly struck them through the absurd

or maybe meaningful. One simply doesn't
know enough, or understand what came
out of the altering weather in a fashioned
descriptive phrase that was common to each name,
or may have surrounded each like a dear frame.

Best not to make much of it and leave these seamen
in the equally altering acre they now have
inherited from strangers though yet human.
They fell from sea to earth, from grave to grave,
and, griefless now, taught others how to grieve.

ROOM FOR LIVING

You should stop here and not step
into that land of strange waters and strange
persuasive drum beats which have power to change
skin and skeleton to an earlier shape
till, like a mumbling cannibal, you set up
your own headstone on a dazzled slope.

These sights trouble your dreams. Like a toothed moon
rearing from rank forest lands you go
in silver aseptic light over the slow
entangled swamps and, as in a bright spoon,
see huge queer shapes dancing: a slant grin
splitting a face as dangerous as a lion.

Nevertheless, if you wish to keep
yourself to yourself and not become
a sort of music beaten on a drum
in a kind of shapelessness and dying sleep
you should stay quietly by this river, not rig ship
to take you down far water, bright and sharp.

If you listen calmly, you can hear music here
of rusted broken strings, an orchestra
that gathers volume like an autumn star
filling your sky with light, stranger more dear
than any light through any atmosphere
of foreign land, nourished by native fear.

A kind of courage glitters in that huge
corrupted music and heroic men
win crippled victories on a staring plain.
If you listen tranquilly you will enlarge
yourself to more than you till the white surge
will bear you also down its stream of courage.

OLD WOMAN

And she, being old, fed from a mashed plate
as an old mare might droop across a fence
to the dull pastures of its ignorance.
Her husband held her upright while he prayed

to God who is all-forgiving to send down
some angel somewhere who might land perhaps
in his foreign wings among the gradual crops.
She munched, half dead, blindly searching the spoon.

Outside, the grass was raging. There I sat
imprisoned in my pity and my shame
that men and women having suffered time
should sit in such a place, in such a state

and wished to be away, yes, to be far away
with athletes, heroes, Greeks or Roman men
who pushed their bitter spears into a vein
and would not spend an hour with such decay.

'Pray God,' he said, 'we ask you, God,' he said.
The bowed back was quiet. I saw the teeth
tighten their grip around a delicate death.
And nothing moved within the knotted head

but only a few poor veins as one might see
vague wishless seaweed floating on a tide
of all the salty waters where had died
too many waves to mark two more or three.

A NOTE ON PURITANS

There was no curtain between them and fire.
Every moment was a moment when
a man could sink into a tranced despair
or shake his heels to vanity and turn
with frenzied gaiety from that drying air.

Therefore their urgency. That fire glowed
along their blackened senses, hour by hour.
Only the book they clutched so tightly cheered
hearts that might stop, eyes that their burning fear
could hole with flame: heads that their thoughts had charred.

Garden and gardener, book and reader glowed:
limbs crackled their sins: silks twitched in a blue flame:
a man's flesh melted in the mouth of God:
he lost his name to earn a lasting name.
A heaven flashed where all that oil flowed.

That was great courage to have watched that fire,
not placing a screen before it as we do
with pictures, poems, landscapes, a great choir
of mounting voices which can drown the raw
hissing and spitting of flame with other fire.

That was great courage to have stayed as true
to truth as man can stay. From them we learn
how certain truths can make men brutish too:
how few can watch the bared teeth slow-burn
and not be touched by the lumps of fire they chew

into contempt and barrenness. I accuse
these men of singleness and loss of grace
who stared so deeply into the fire's hues
that all was fire to them.
                              Yes, to this place
they should return. Cheeks have the fire men choose.

15

SCHOOLGIRL ON SPEECHDAY
IN THE OPEN AIR

Here in their health and youth they're sitting down
on thick tight grass while bald official men
heavy with sunshine wear a moment's crown
and put it by reluctantly again.

I look at one who lies upon her side
wearing bright yellow for the clasping light.
No ring of shadow has engaged her pride
or wolfed her, fallen, in the circling night.

Her scorn springs out like swords. A smile plays round
her unstained lips as if a joke might spill.
She turns her shining head into that sound
which stumbles downward from low hill to hill.

And then I turn again and see how one
dangles her will from every word he spins
and think how thirty years can fence a man
by what he loses and by what he wins

into a little ground where he can see
the golden landlords, pursed with luck, stride past
and schoolgirls, flashing by, are far and free
as fish he played for but new men will taste.

And the timed applause which falls from rock to rock
and then to silence is the way he came.
She gathers like necessity her cloak.
The schoolgirl rises—and must do the same.

DYING IS NOT SETTING OUT

Dying is not setting out
in a full flower of sails.
More complex ropes are taut
across the blue pulse.

Dying is not like sailing
by the shores of Mull or
Tiree. Sheet's less willing
and twists in thick air.

It's not for Skye we make.
Not with simple hands
use south wind for luck.
We wear our islands

unconnected in spite of
intellect's glittering stride.
We sail into the grave
of the more than dead.

ABOUT THAT MILE

'It all grew in a garden, all that sin,'
said he with his tormented face.
'You ask me for the meaning of our pain
and the thick darkness boiling with God's grace.
You ask me how a shining moral knife
cuts apples into slices like a housewife.

You ask me why Satan like a malcontent
enters our plays and always steals the show
dressed in his bitter black, most eloquent
to speak of slavery and the way we grow
aslant into the wind, like bending corn.
As if the evil lay in being born.

You ask me why a helpless child should die
in speechless agony, or a woman drag
her cancer like a creel, or how an eye
must stare unblinking on a hanging rag
to find the flesh beneath it: or the reason
for such a death as sucks us like a passion

down to the briny dregs. All these you ask.
And why two people living in a mile
of perfume and vast leisure failed their task.
And why across that innocence and smile,
a stinging whip spoke savagely from space
across the mortal and decaying face.

Yet I, like you, have heartbreaks of my own.
I die of no ideas but of men.
You think me moral like the weighted stone
engraved on graves. Yet you take your pen
and write a poem in the space you fear.
Could you do this if space were everywhere?

You ask me this. I am not God,' he said.
'I build my fence nor do I say I can
hit every nail exactly on the head
not even those nails which drove the Son of Man
deeper against the wood. I munch my way
across these pastures till the edge of day.'

'About that mile,' I said, 'about that mile
you talked of there.' 'Well,' he pursued, 'what then?'
'Do you not,' I questioned with a half-smile,
'dream of it sometimes, wish it back again?'
But he with an equal smile said then to me:
'I turn to poetry for such foolery.'

SUNDAY MORNING WALK

Sunday of wrangling bells—and salt in the air—
I passed the tall black men and their women walking
over the tight-locked streets which were all on fire
with summer ascendant. The seas were talking and talking

as I took my way to the wood where the river ran quiet.
The grass lay windowed in sunlight, the leaves were raging
in furious dying green. The road turned right
round the upstanding castle whose stone, unaging,

marks how a world remains as I, being now
pack of a wandering flesh, take holiday, strolling
far from the churches' declaiming. Health will allow
riots of naiads and nymphs, so wantonly rolling

18

with me in leaves in woods, thinking how once
Jove took his pleasure of Leda or—splendid embracing—
god would mate with a goddess—rapid the pounce,
fruitful the hot-thighed meeting, no need for unlacing.

And occupied thus, I came where a dead sheep lay
close to a fence, days gone. The flies were hissing and buzzing
out of the boiling eyes, wide open as day.
I stood in the sunlight beside it, watching and musing.

Three crows famished yards off. Live sheep grazed far
from the rotting carcass. The jaw, well-shaved, lay slackly
there on the warm quiet grass. The household air
was busy with buzzing like fever. How quickly, how quickly

the wool was peeled from the back! How still was the flesh!
How the visiting flies would not knock at the door of the sockets!
How the hole in the side gaped red, a well-sized gash!
How the clear young lambs grazed in the shade of the thickets!

And the sun blazed hot on my shoulder. Here was no shade.
But the sheep was quiet, so quiet. There was nothing to notice
but the grape-bunched flies and the crows. Could a world have stayed
if I'd taken a stick in my hand to beat off the flies!

They would merely return when I'd gone and busy as always
inhabit this larder again no matter how brightly
I struck with my smart sharp stick. All I could praise—
yes, all I could praise—was the sheep lying there so quietly

not knowing, not knowing. High summer was raging around.
I stood in my slack clean clothes. The stones were burning.
The flies in the wound continued their occupied sound
as I turned my back on a death of no weeping or mourning.

(3)

The day's in love with you as suns with gardens.
The dappled shade shakes thought across your brow.
If this is prison you spread out your pardons
for all dark sentences we suffer now.

You govern guilt by innocence, and dungeons
open like leaves to green and cool keys,
the twisted inmates straighten like a conscience
and by your glance all shufflers stand at ease.

And all the darkness gathers light about it
to hide its devilish shame as devils do.
If this is heresy can devils doubt it
who've made their best theology of you.

No mineral in your earth to tempt to stealing:
such tender shadows merely can provoke
the longing for a perfectness of feeling
we've almost spoken but we never spoke.

For only at rarest moments can we scent it
the garden we have lost but cannot find
and you the shining page that clearly meant it
already turn to print across the mind.

(4)

I know a young girl of great wit
who walks like Venus in her stylish gait
and some would say 'Conceit' but I would say:
'A sun contents us if the clouds are grey,'
and also, 'Have you seen between the stones
the water running as the water runs?'

All things that speak of surety and grace
proclaim us heretic from our proper place
though venomous devils preach against the light
which opens heavens at her precious feet.
Yet even these by sneers and laughs make known
the dear theology they now disown.

20

from LOVE SONGS OF A PURITAN (B)

(3)

The piper, marching in his peacock style
and proud obsession with his accurate notes,
brings cheering children to the flaring streets
to follow ribbons, bonnets, myths of steel.
Yet few who watch him see how fingers twirl
as fast as spinning on a tuneful loom
or a mind's motion or a delicate girl,
fencing with love that growing will consume.

And you, like him, wear inner style though some
be most attracted to the outward show
of face and motion, grace and perfect limb,
as if theology, the devil's foe,
should tell us only of the outward dream,
not stylish maker playing here below.

(8)

Searching yourself to find a saving God
is flashing torchlight in a wavering room
where darkness eats the hand, and every word
lies vased in paper on a huddled tomb.
Whatever's seen is what the light makes known
shaking in fingers dying of despair,
its light will not curve round you to make noon,
you in the centre seeing everywhere.

But straight ahead is all the torch can show
devouring darkness with a trembling line.
Behind you devils mumble, monsters grow
their sniggering shadows leeching blood like wine.
All that the torch reveals is where you go
not whether roads are devilish or divine.

BY FERRY TO THE ISLAND

We crossed by ferry to the bare island
where sheep and cows stared coldly through the wind—
the sea behind us with its silver water,
the silent ferryman standing in the stern
clutching his coat about him like old iron.

We landed from the ferry and went inland
past a small church down to the winding shore
where a white seagull fallen from the failing
chill and ancient daylight lay so pure
and softly breasted that it made more dear

the lesser white around us. There we sat,
sheltered by a rock beside the sea.
Someone made coffee, someone played the fool
in a high rising voice for two hours.
The sea's language was more grave and harsh.

And one sat there whose dress was white and cool.
The fool sparkled his wit that she might hear
new diamonds turning on her naked finger.
What might the sea think or the dull sheep
lifting its head through heavy Sunday sleep?

And later, going home, a moon rising
at the end of a cart-track, minimum of red,
the wind being dark, imperfect cows staring
out of their half-intelligence, and a plough
lying on its side in the cold, raw

naked twilight, there began to move
slowly, like heavy water, in the heart
the image of the gull and of that dress,
both being white and out of the darkness rising
the moon ahead of us with its rusty ring.

from HIGHLAND PORTRAIT

Country of céilidhs and the delicate manners,
obstinate dowagers of emerald honours,
the rain has worn your metaphors away.
Only poor rays of similes are shining
from brooches and from buckles. The complaining
barren rooks and ravens fill the day.

Nothing to say except a world has ended.
The waters of Polldubh, direct and splendid,
will hump unsteady men to a boiling death.
Yet from the shaking bridge of fascination
we see in these the antiseptic passion
whose surgeon's reason is a kind of birth.

A YOUNG HIGHLAND GIRL
STUDYING POETRY

Poetry drives its lines into her forehead
like an angled plough across a bare field.
I've seen her kind before, of the live and dead
who bore humped creels when the beating winds were wild.

Nor did they know much poetry but were skilful
at healing children, bringing lambs to birth.
The earth they lived from did not make them soulful.
The foreign rose abated at their mouth.

Yet they were dancers too and feared the season
when 'pale Orion shook the seas with fire.'
Peculiar waters had their inner reasons
for curing wastrels of a mental star.

And she—like them—should grow along these valleys
bearing bright children, being kind to love.
Simple affection needs no complex solace
‚nor quieter minds abstractions of the grave.

For most must walk though some by natural flying
learn from the bitter winds a kind of praise.
These fruits are different. She will know one dying
but he by many deaths will bless her days.

23

HOME

To have to stay
in spite of scorn, hatred,
in spite of shattered
illusions also. To be unable
to break cleanly away
since this is truly home
simple, imperishable,
since otherwhere is chill,
dull-breasted, dumb.

Since this too is hated,
loved, willed to be perfect, willed
to a finer yield,
fiercer, less barren, richer,
its harvests be completed.
Since to have seen tall men
moving in light and fire
yet human too is more
grace than can be given

this (one says) is tragic
(to be fixed on a wheel
implacable, internal,
as tears break, as roses
bowed gravely down to rock
proliferate endless versions)
is not tragic but cause
of fresh honours, horses
impelled by used reins.

STUDIES IN POWER

(1)

Today at a meeting while I sat confused
by motions, counter-motions, and the vague
appalling ardour of the dialogue
I was struck by terror (being thus bemused)
that I (O certainly no albatross
of a dear unearthly climate) should be there,
somehow a stranger, at a total loss
(no, not uncommon, let me be quite clear)

till this fear struck me with a dizzy force
that this was real and the poems I make
mere cardboard coins to fill a childish purse.

And I was terrified lest my world be fake
and these blunt men who make all words opaque
should stand like giants by my dwarfish verse.

(2)

I thought of power and its sources while
the table trembled under a bronze thought
and men grew marble of a dreaming sort
all round me even here. Mile upon mile
the violent and the beautiful strode on
one in her deadly silks, the other in
black Roman leather with the brassy belt
and both impervious to my senseless guilt.

Til suddenly there I saw a vase in bloom
gathering light about it clearly clearly
in adult daylight not by a moon obscurely,

and its harder language filled the small room
with its bare constant self, its paradigm
of straining forces harmonised sincerely.

25

from LILAC, SNOW AND SHADOW

(1)

A lilac dress casting a long shadow
on a patch of bright snow.
The skies pass by in blue, in blue marching.

O dear my country that you give me these,
lilac on snow, the urgent turbulent skies,
me walking at ease the supple air inhaling.

O dear my island with the seas around you
I kneel this moment to the innumerable dead,
who have fed dense waters and the blue Aprils,

for these simplicities of a complex air,
a lilac dress, the snow, the blue sky marching,
myself of a hundred colours swarming there.

(2)

I think of my friends, of sixteen years' silence,
in their blue tunics, nagged by the blue waves.

Their ships written in gold on slanted caps.
What was the meaning of their vigorous dying?

Of the long guns retracting after thunder,
the golden admirals in their cosy braid:

of their dread bodies fished by the tactful sun:
and I impelled by lilacs and this snow?

II

OLD WOMAN

Your thorned back
heavily under the creel
you steadily stamped the rising daffodil.

Your set mouth
forgives no-one, not even God's justice
perpetually drowning law with grace.

Your cold eyes
watched your drunken husband come
unsteadily from Sodom home.

Your grained hands
dandled full and sinful cradles.
You built for your children stone walls.

Your yellow hair
burned slowly in a scarf of grey
wildly falling like the mountain spray.

Finally, you're alone
among the unforgiving brass,
the slow silences, the sinful glass.

Who never learned,
not even aging, to forgive
our poor journey and our common grave,

while the free daffodils
wave in the valleys and on the hills
the deer look down with their instinctive skills,

and the huge seas
in which your brothers drowned sing slow
over the headland and the peevish crow.

OLD HIGHLAND LADY READING NEWSPAPER

Grasping the newspaper in kneaded hands
in her ordered bed, the tablets at the side,
she slowly reads of all her friends who've died
in the black holds of the approaching islands

where the horses and the daffodils are dead,
unfashionable skirts have swirled away
down the Dutch cornfields and the fields of hay
into the numerous caves of her bald head

bent over print and old remorseless hands
grasping these deaths, the tombstones all in white
her eyes traverse with gritty appetite
in the slow justice of her mouth's small sounds.

FACE OF AN OLD HIGHLAND WOMAN

This face is not the Mona Lisa's
staring from a submarine
greenness of water. There's no grace
of any Renaissance on the skin

but rocks slowly thrust through earth
a map with the wind going over stone
beyond the mercies of Nazareth.
Here is the God of fist and bone

a complex twisted Testament
two eyes like lochs staring up
from heather gnarled by a bare wind
beyond the art and dance of Europe.

IT IS THE OLD

It is the old
who get up in the night to build the fires for the young.
Their gods, they imagine, are disposed
in a leisurely lazy heaven and prolong
a Norman sleep against the cold
and bitter frost.

And so they set
a delicate structure of sticks, enfolded in this
fear of their power, idolatry of their poise.
Not knowing in Saxon dawns how the abyss
their precarious tilt of sticks steadily lights
is what their boys

dread in their beds,
while dreaming of lords they can serve
of brilliance courage and wit.
Roads are built on each nerve—
Roman and servile and powerful. Their needs
point to the fire in the night.

TWO GIRLS SINGING

It neither was the words nor yet the tune.
Any tune would have done and any words.
Any listener or no listener at all.

As nightingales in rocks or a child crooning
in its own world of strange awakening
or larks for no reason but themselves.

So on the bus through late November running
by yellow lights tormented, darkness falling,
the two girls sang for miles and miles together

and it wasn't the words or tune. It was the singing.
It was the human sweetness in that yellow,
the unpredicted voices of our kind.

LENIN

In a chair of iron
sits coldly my image of Lenin,
that troubling man
'who never read a book for pleasure alone.'

The germ inside the sealed train
emerged, spread in wind and rain
into new minds in revolution
seeming more real than had been,

for instance, Dostoevsky. No, I can
romanticise no more that 'head of iron,'
'the thought and will unalterably one,'
'the word-doer,' 'thunderer,' 'the stone

rolling through clouds.' Simple to condemn
the unsymmetrical, simple to condone
that which oneself is not. By admiration
purge one's envy of unadult iron

when the true dialectic is to turn
in the infinitely complex, like a chain
we steadily burn through, steadily forge and burn
not to be dismissed in any poem

by admiration for the ruthless man
nor for the saint but for the moving on
into the endlessly various, real, human,
world which is no new era, shining dawn.

JOHNSON IN THE HIGHLANDS

A reasoning mind travels through this country.
In these sad wastes a Londoner by choice
sees water falling, and some meagre deer.

Examines with his tough reasoning mind
lochs, deer, and people: is not seduced
by Mrs Radcliffe's green hysteria

from a musical prose we've never once achieved,
whose fences cannot reach between the words
whose arguments are broken-backed with exile.

A classical sanity considers Skye.
A huge hard light falls across shifting hills.
This mind, contemptuous of miracles

and beggarly sentiment, illuminates
a healthy moderation. But I hear
like a native dog notes beyond his range

the modulations of a queer music
twisting his huge black body in the pain
that shook him also in raw blazing London.

THE CLEARANCES

The thistles climb the thatch. Forever
this sharp scale in our poems,
as also the waste music of the sea.

The stars shine over Sutherland
in a cold ceilidh of their own,
as, in the morning, the silver cane

cropped among corn. We will remember this.
Though hate is evil we cannot
but hope your courtier's heels in hell

are burning: that to hear
the thatch sizzling in tanged smoke
your hot ears slowly learn.

AT THE FIRTH OF LORNE

In the cold orange light we stared across
to Mull and Kerrera and far Tiree.
A setting sun emblazoned your bright knee
to a brilliant gold to match your hair's gold poise.

Nothing had changed: the world was as it was
a million years ago. The slaty stone
slept in its tinged and aboriginal iron.
The sky might flower a little, and the grass

perpetuate its sheep. But from the sea
the bare bleak islands rose, beyond the few
uneasy witticisms we let pursue
their desolate silences. There was no tree

nor other witness to the looks we gave
each other there, inhuman as if tolled
by some huge bell of iron and of gold,
I no great Adam and you no bright Eve.

THE LAW AND THE GRACE

It's law they ask of me and not grace.
'Conform,' they say, 'your works are not enough.
Be what we say you should be,' even if
graceful hypocrisy obscures my face.

'We know no angels. If you say you do
that's blasphemy and devilry.' Yet I have
known some bright angels, of spontaneous love.
Should I deny them, be to falsehood true,

the squeeze of law which has invented torture
to bring the grace to a malignant head?
Do you want me, angels, to be wholly dead?
Do you need, black devils, steadfastly to cure

life of itself? And you to stand beside
the stone you set on me? No, I have angels. Mine
are free and perfect. They have no design
on anyone else, but only on my pride,

my insufficiency, imperfect works.
They often leave me but they sometimes come
to judge me to the core, till I am dumb.
Is this not law enough, you patriarchs?

THE CEMETERY NEAR BURNS'
COTTAGE

Tombs of the Covenanters nod together
grey heads and obstinate. They saw them come
the silver horsemen meditating murder
but stood there quietly to the beating drum
of God and psalm, the heart's immaculate order.

So now I see them as the churchyard turns
red in the evening light. They did not know
that moral milk turns sour, and something churns
inside the stony cask. This churchyard now
flickers with light, untameably with Burns,

the secret enemy within the stone,
the hand which even here stings its hot whip
in glittering rays from socketed bone to bone.
In such fixed Eden did his changing shape
unlock their teeth from what they'd bravely won.

HUME

More than this I do not love you,
Hume of the reasonable mind.
There was an otter crossed the sound,
a salmon in his cold teeth.

The mist came down. Between two capes
there was no road. There was a French
salon, an adoring wench.
He picked the salmon with his teeth.

Delicate Hume who swims through all
the daring firths of broken Scotland,
there were no roads across the land.
The causes, like old fences, yawned

gravely over wit and port.
Diplomacies are what displace
the inner law, the inner grace,
the Corrievreckan of bad art.

36

PREPARATION FOR A DEATH

Have I seen death conquered at last in you
dying by inches, yet with lucid sight
examining its gains? The world was new
and sparkled with a gay Renaissance wit,

but now the Reformation has set in.
A narrow Luther hedges the red blood
and bellows from his pulpit like a pain.
The blossoming angels in their painted red

are withered into devils. All the pardons
are snatched inhospitably from your open wound
and nothing's left but a creeping host of sins
which you consider with a bleak mind

on the very edge of nothingness looking out,
like Drake going off beyond all human shores
and no Elizabeth to dub you knight
but mind itself to open its black doors.

ENCOUNTER IN A SCHOOL CORRIDOR

Supposing today walking along this passage
in a flicker of gown Death were to turn and look
with his white skull face, raising his eyes from his book,
and I were to stare directly into that visage

which is almost over-learned and frightened too
as if to say: 'Surely not you as well.'
In this hygienic place without sound or smell
what would I, late cold Roman, say or do

but this perhaps: 'Always there was correction.
After the Fall, the careless summer leaves
must learn strict order, for the heart deceives
by wayward and incurious affection.

And the seasons always begin. There is no end
to the iron ring of law, the field of grace
whose shadows slant before the footballers.'
He then might show some pity as he turned

37

to face me down the dim-lit corridor
his arms so piled with books, face grained with thought,
and his slow legs remembering that riot
of flowering shadows and that youthful force.

TO FORGET THE DEAD

To forget the dead. How to forget the dead
when they slowly sigh, walking about the rooms
where we are lying, deep in a white bed.
How to forget that with discoloured arms

they are searching drawers for their property—
a favourite ribbon, book—while we lie still
under the bedclothes lest they hear us cry,
and stuffing sheets in our round mouths, till

we are the dead, swathed in our tight linen,
and those who leave no shadow in the glass
stand at the door a moment, but refrain
from touching our white gravestones as they pass.

THE CHESS PLAYER

When the badness came he was playing chess again.
'Someone most dear to you,' they said, 'has died.'
He scouted round the board and picked the queen.
(What use are bishops, knights?) 'We found,' they cried,
'your brother dead. His wounds were in the side.'

'Not in the head?' he said, not looking up.
'In the head and heart as well,' they answered. He
moved the tall queen delicately as in hope
but the king escaped again. 'Did he say of me
anything hopeful?' he asked savagely,

moving a pawn, his head carved to the wood
the king was carved from. 'No,' they said. '"Please tell
my brother this. Tell him I've understood
a very little." That's what he told us.' 'Well,
The chessboard tells me what of heaven or hell

I need to know and that's too much,' he cried,
shifting the queen. (The king escaped again.)
He smiled a little with the jaunty pride
one sometimes notices in desperate men.
'You see,' he said, 'when you came in just then

I had a vision of that very board.
They do not know, you see, none of them knows.
They're all quite evidently so far apart.
What do they know of each other? I dispose—
but each is wooden, in archaic pose.'

And then they saw (each one standing beside
the terrible trivial wrestler) with a start
that someone most dear to him indeed had died,
and stared at him grappling with his mental art,
and carefully made ready to depart.

THE SONG

'Never again will we part.' So says the song.
So why should the heart be downcast when it hears
what for so many years it has learnt to long
for, most and tenderly. Why should the hours

suddenly seem to freeze on the clock
in their black monuments? And why should you
sit in the happy ending like a rock
when the sea and sky around you are so blue?

ENVOI

Remember me when you come into your kingdom.
Remember me, beggar of mirrors, when you are confirmed
in the sleep of fulfilment on the white pillow.

Remember me who knock at the window,
who hirple on my collapsing stick, and know
the quivering northern lights of nerves.

Remember me in your good autumn.
I in my plates of frost go
among the falling crockery of hills,

stones, plains, all falling and falling.
In my winter of the sick glass remember
me in your autumn, in your good sleep.

from WORLD WAR ONE

(2)

They droop out of the twilight, slack-rifled,
their eyes tired to stone, their bayonets green.
Around them, an insane loom of light.

A letter winks from a cold pocket.
"Dear Son," "Dear Bill." (A house made of bone
furrows an unmitigated distance.)

Laces trail. This is a sky of heroes
where the small birds are too awed to sing.
Kettles boil in the depths of heads.

Sleepwalking, they pass our tall statues.
Poppies fall on their heads. They don't halt
They march under the foam of speeches.

As if they're tired. As if they don't see.
Nevertheless their eyes are open.
Strangely in the noise one fixes bayonet,

charges. The blade sinks in wreaths.
He screams onward like a train
through the green pastures of England.

(5)

NOVEMBER 1961

I can't cry for these men.
Their physical wrestling is too strange
for the purer boil that stirs my pen.
They're like the stones of Stonehenge

staggering about blind fields.
The shrill needles of our minds
pierce deeper. There are no shields
either of steel or of diamonds

to jam their craft. Even in the silence
unresting jabbing points hem
a dress composed of violence
and stunned peace. A dry flame

worse perhaps than the physical
burns their untidiness away
from the private to the general
debt that our feelings cannot pay.

DEER ON THE HIGH HILLS—
A MEDITATION

I

A deer looks through you to the other side,
and what it is and sees is an inhuman pride.

II

Yesterday three deer stood at the roadside.
It was icy January and there they were
like debutantes on a smooth ballroom floor.

They stared at us out of that French
arrogant atmosphere, like Louis the Sixteenth
sustained in twilight on a marble plinth.

They wore the inhuman look of aristocrats
before a revolution comes, and the people
blaspheme the holy bells in the high steeple.

Before the ice breaks, and heroes in spring
come up like trees with bursting wrongs in their arms
and feed the nobles to the uniform worms.

So were these deer, balanced on delicate logic,
till suddenly they broke from us and went
outraged and sniffing into the dark wind.

Difficult to say where they go to
in the harsh weather when the mountains stand
like judging elders, tall on either hand.

Except that they know the ice is breaking now.
They take to the hills pursued by darkness and lie
beneath the starry metaphysical sky.

Sometimes in a savage winter they'll come down
and beg like fallen nobles for their bread.
They'd rather live in poverty than be dead.

Nevertheless there's something dangerous
in a deer's head. He might suddenly open your belly
with his bitter antlers to the barren sky.

Especially in winter when tormented
by loneliness they descend to this road
with great bounding leaps like the mind of God.

In summer they can be ignored. They crop so gently
among the hills that no-one notices
their happy heads sunk in the feeding cresses.

But beware of them now when ice is on the ground.
A beggared noble can conceal a sword
next to his skin for the aimless and abhorred

tyrants who cannot dance but throw stones,
tyrants who can crack the finest bones:
tyrants who do not wear but break most ancient crowns.

III

One would be finished with these practical things
in order to return as deer do
to the tall mountain springs.

Nevertheless one should not so return
till soldier of the practical or doer
one wholly learns to learn

a real contempt, a fine hard-won disdain
for these possessions, marbles of unripe children,
as, again,

a deer might walk along a sweating street
stare in a cramped window and then go
back to the hills but not on ignorant feet.

IV

Forget these purple evenings and these poems
that solved all or took for myth
and pointed sail of Ulysses enigmatic.

43

There was Hector with his child in his arms.
Where is that other Hector
who wore the internal shield, the inner sword?

Ulysses scurries, like a rat trapped in a maze.
He wears the sharp look of a business magnate.
Late from the office he had a good excuse.

Ideas clash on the mountain tops.
By the appalled peaks the deer roar.
Simply a question of rutting, these cloudy systems

or as yesterday we saw a black cloud
become the expression of a tall mountain.
And that was death, the undertaker, present.

And all became like it for that moment,
assumption of anguish, and the hollow waters
the metaphysics of an empty country

deranged, deranged, a land of rain and stones,
of stones and rain, of the huge barbarous bones,
plucked like a loutish harp their harmonies.

V

You must build from the rain and stones,
from the incurable numbers: the grasses
innumerable on the many hills.

Not to geometry or algebra,
or an inhuman music, but
in the hollow roar of the waterfall,

you must build from there and not be
circumvented by sunlight or a taste of love
or intuitions from the sky above

the deadly rock. Or even history,
Prince Charles in a gay Highland shawl,
or mystery in a black Highland coffin.

You must build from the rain and stones
till you can make
a stylish deer on the high hills,
and let its leaps be unpredictable!

VI

Duncan Ban McIntyre, the poet,
knew them intimately, was one of them.
They had waxen hides, they were delicate dancers.

They evolved their own music which became
his music: they elected him
their poet laureate.

It was a kind of Eden these days
with something Cretan in his eulogy.
Nevertheless he shot them also.

Like shooting an image or a vivid grace.
Brutality and beauty danced together
in a silver air, incorruptible.

And the clean shot did not disturb his poems.
Nor did the deer kneel in a pool of tears.
The stakes were indeed high in that game.

And the rocks did not weep with sentiment.
They were simply there: the deer were simply there.
The witty gun blazed from his knowing hand.

VII

What is the knowledge of the deer?
Is there a philosophy of the hills?
Do their heads peer into the live stars?

Do rumours of death disturb them? They do not live
by local churchyards, hotels or schools.
They inhabit wild systems.

Do they outface winds or lie down
in warm places? Winter, interrogant,
displaces spring and summer, undulant.

Their horns have locked in blood. Yes, their horns
have gored bellies. The dainty hind
has absolute passion, similar and proud.

It is not evil makes the horns bright
but a running natural lustre. The blood
is natural wounding. Metaphoric sword

is not their weapon, but an honest thrust.
Nor does the moon affect their coupling, nor
remonstrant gods schoolmaster their woods.

Evil not intentional, but desire
disturbs to battle. The great spring is how
these savage captains tear to indigo

the fiery guts. Evil's more complex, is
a languaged metaphor, like the mists that scarf
the deadly hind and her bewildered calf.

VIII

Supposing God had a branched head like this
considering Himself in a pool.
It is not the image of the beautiful

makes it so, simply as in a mirror,
but in its fadingness, as on the ice
the deer might suddenly slip, go suddenly under,

their balance being precarious. It is this,
that makes her beautiful, she who now obscures
unconscious heavens with her conscious ray,

is concourse of bright flesh, sad, is remembering
herself so going, so implacable,
her failing voyages to the obstinate rocks:

as deer so stand, precarious, of a style,
half-here, half-there, a half-way lustre breaking
a wise dawn in a chained ocean far.

As dear, so dear, Vesuvius, rocket, you
being ice and water, winter and summer, take
the mountainous seas into your small logic.

God may not be beautiful, but you
suffer a local wound. You bleed to death
from all that's best, your active anima.

The deer and you may well be beautiful,
for through your bones as through a mathematics
concordant honouring beauty richly breaks.

IX

Deer on the high peaks, calling, calling,
you speak of love, love of the mind and body.
Your absolute heads populate the hills

like daring thoughts, half-in, half-out this world,
as a lake might open, and a god peer
into a room where failing darkness glows.

Deer on the high peaks, there have been heads
as proud as yours, destructive, ominous,
of an impetuous language, measureless.

Heads like yours, so scrutinous and still,
yet venomed too with the helpless thrust of spring,
so magisterial, violent, yet composed:

heads of a thirsty intellect, sensuous as
the thirst of bellies in a summer day
July and waspish, on a murmuring ground.

Heads like valleys where the stars fed,
unknown and magical, strange and unassuaged,
the harmonies humming in a green place.

So proud these heads, original, distinct,
they made an air imperial around
their pointed scrutiny, passionate with power.

Electric instinct of the high hills
till, later, later peasants in the valleys
felt in their bones disquieting kingdoms break

and matrons, by small cottages, would sense
implacable navies in their native wombs,
a generation of a harder wit

and later later when the senses quickened
(the hills being bare again) in a new season
in a night honoured with a desperate star

47

another head appeared, fiercer than these,
disdain flashed from his horns, a strange cry
perplexed the peasants, somnolent, appeased.

X

Deer on the high peaks, the wandering senses
are all, are all: fanatic heads deceive,
like branches springing in a true desert.

Smell now the cresses and the winter root,
passage of heather, journey of rank fox
mortal and moving on the strange hills.

In spring the raven and lascivious swallow,
migrant of air, the endless circle closing,
unclosing, closing, a bewildering ring

of natural marriage, pagan, sensuous.
Return of seasons, and the fugitive
Culloden of scents, erratic, hesitant.

The snow returning, and the summer wasp
more caustic than idea, hum of bees
at their devotions to the wild honey.

The hind crowned with her wanton sex,
rage of the sap in trees, the urgent salmon
pregnant with oceans dying into streams.

And these return in spite of the idea,
the direct reasoning road, the mad Ulysses
so unperverted, so implacable,

so wearing late his dull ironic crown
among a people he has never loved
nor felt in boredom kinship ominous

but fixed on a reasoned star his obstinate gaze
who came at last to where his childhood was
an infant island in an ancient place.

XI

Deer on the high peaks, let me turn
my gaze far from you, where the river winds
its slow way like an old man's argument.

The rocks obstinate, the rains persistent,
the stones ingathered into their chastened fury,
all things themselves, a fierce diversity.

The rampant egos of the flat plains,
the thorns gentle with their sour flowers,
tongues of the sharp stones, the water's business.

Contorted selves that twist in a dark wind,
far from the mountains, from the far and clear
ordered inventions of the stars ongoing.

And here, below, the water's business
smoothing the stone, consenting to the heads
that, easy of a summer, stare and stare

and speak: 'I am, I am. Preserve me, O preserve.
Make me in mirror matchless and the earl
of such imagined kingdoms as endure.

I pray, I pray, a marchioness of this
dismembered kingdom, let my face be seen
not mortal now but of a lasting grace.'

Roar of the waters, prickly thrust of thorn,
immutable stone, sand of a brute fact,
these are the maenads of necessity.

And the deer look down, Platonic dawn breaks
on Highland hills as distant as a thought,
an excellent Athens, obstinate mirage,

while the stone rears, the venomed stone rears
its savage being, and the waters pour
illusive summers to the real seas,

while the deer stand imperious, of a style,
make vibrant music, high and rich and clear,
mean what the plain mismeans, inform a chaos.

XII

Deer on the high hills, in your halfway kingdom,
uneasy in this, uneasy in the other,
but all at ease when earth and sky together

are mixed are mixed, become a royalty
none other knows, neither the migrant birds
nor the beasts chained to their instinctive courses.

That halfway kingdom is your royalty,
you on a meditative truth impaled,
the epicures of feeding absolutes,

you of a metaphysics still and proud,
native to air, native to earth both,
indigenous deer beneath a cloudburst sky;

to whom the lightning's native and the thunder,
whose sockets flash with an annunciant fire,
whose storms are vegetation's dearest friend.

Your antlers flash in light, your speed like thought
is inspiration decorous and assured,
a grace not theological but of

accomplished bodies, sensuous and swift,
of summer scents enjoyers, and of winters
the permanent spirits, watchful, unappeased:

of summer hills a speaking radiance
the body's language, excellent and pure,
discoursing love, free as the wandering wind:

of scentless winters the philosophers,
vigilant always like a tiptoe mind
on peaks of sorrow, brave and scrutinous:

on peaks of sorrow, brave and scrutinous,
on breakneck peaks, coherent and aplomb,
the image silent on the high hill.

XIII

Do colours cry? Does 'black' weep for the dead?
Is green so bridal, and is red the flag
and eloquent elegy of a martial sleep?

Are hills 'majestic' and devoted stones
plotting in inner distances our fall?
The mind a sea: and she a Helen who

in budding hours awakens to her new
enchanting empire all the summer day,
the keys of prisons dangling in her hands?

Is night a woman, and the moon a queen
or dowager of grace, and all the stars
archaic courtiers round ambiguous smiles?

Are rivers stories, and are plains their prose?
Are fountains poetry? And are rainbows the
wistful smiles upon a dying face?

And you, the deer, who walk upon the peaks,
are you a world away, a language distant?
Such symbols freeze upon my desolate lips!

XIV

There is no metaphor. The stone is stony.
The deer step out in isolated air.
We move at random on an innocent journey.

The rain is rainy and the sun is sunny.
The flower is flowery and the sea is salty.
My friend himself, himself my enemy.

The deer step out in isolated air.
Not nobles now but of a further journey.
Their flesh is distant as the air is airy.

The rivers torrents, and the grasses many.
The stars are starry, and the night nocturnal.
The fox a tenant of no other skin.

51

Who brings reports? There's one head to the penny.
A door is wooden, and no window grieves
for lovers turned away, for widows lonely.

The deer step out in isolated air.
The cloud is cloudy and the word is wordy.
Winter is wintry, lonely is your journey.

'You called sir did you?' 'I who was so lonely
would speak with you: would speak to this tall chair,
would fill it chock-full of my melancholy.'

So being lonely I would speak with any
stone or tree or river. Bear my journey,
you endless water, dance with a human joy.

This distance deadly! God or goddess throw me
a rope to landscape, let that hill, so bare,
blossom with grapes, the wine of Italy.

The deer step out in isolated air.
Forgive the distance, let the transient journey
on delicate ice not tragical appear

for stars are starry and the rain is rainy,
the stone is stony, and the sun is sunny,
the deer step out in isolated air.

III

from BIOBUILL IS SANASAN REICE
(Bibles and Advertisements)

YOUNG GIRL

Young girl who goes with a straight back on the street, there are baskets of flowers in my breast, my table is furnished with your laughter.

A woman will say to me, 'There is pride in her walk.' But I will answer as is fitting, 'Is there pride in the sun in the sky? Is there jealousy between the stone and the gold?'

And when a storm goes past in its own world of rain and wind will you say, 'Pride and arrogance' to it, as it turns forests upside down?

Will you speak disparagingly of the diamond because of its glitter or the sea because of its radiance? There is a white ship among the boats and among the black hats there is a crown.

YOU ARE AT THE BOTTOM OF MY MIND

Without my knowing it you are at the bottom of my mind, like one who visits the bottom of the sea with his helmet and his two great eyes: and I do not know properly your expression or your manner after five years of the showers of time pouring between you and me.

Nameless mountains of water pouring between me, hauling you on board, and your expression and manner in my weak hands. You went astray among the mysterious foliage of the sea-bottom in the green half-light without love.

And you will never rise to the surface of the sea, even though my hands should be ceaselessly hauling, and I do not know your way at all, you in the half-light of your sleep, haunting the bottom of the sea without ceasing, and I hauling and hauling on the surface of the ocean.

GOING HOME

Tomorrow I will go home to my island, trying to put a world into forgetfulness. I will lift a fistful of its earth in my hands or I will sit on a hillock of the mind, watching 'the shepherd with his sheep.'

There will ascend (I presume) a thrush. A dawn or two will rise. A boat will be lying in the glitter of the western sun: and water will be running through the world of the similes of my intelligence.

But I will be thinking (in spite of that) of the great fire that is behind our thoughts, Nagasaki and Hiroshima, and I will hear in a room by myself a ghost or two constantly moving, the ghost of every error, the ghost of every guilt, the ghost of each time I walked past the wounded man on the stony road, the ghost of nothingness scrutinising my dumb room with distant face till the island is an ark rising and falling on a great sea and no one knowing whether the dove will ever return, and people talking and talking to each other, and the rainbow of forgiveness in their tears.

TO AN OLD WOMAN

You are in the church listening, sitting on an uncomfortable bench to the words of one who is only half your age.

And I am sitting here writing these corrupted words, and not knowing whether it is the truth or the beautiful lie that is in my mind.

But there is one person who comes into my mind, you sitting in front of a pulpit in your simple black hat, and in your coat (black as well) and in your shoes that have walked many a long street with you.

You were not a scholar in your day. (Many a morning did you gut herring, and your hands were sore with salt, and the keen wind on the edge of your knife, and your fingers frozen with fire.)

You have never heard of Darwin or Freud or Marx or that other Jew, Einstein, with the brilliant mind: nor do you know the meaning of the dream you dreamed last night in your room in heavy sleep.

You haven't heard how the stars move away from us like calm queens through the sky. And you haven't heard how the lion with his fierce head sits at the table with us.

But you sit there in front of the pulpit and in your loneliness you say many a prayer and if the minister shakes you by the hand your mind is filled with happiness.

You remember other days, a sermon direct as a bullet, a summer pouring around a church, a gold ring and the testimony of roses opening summer like a new Bible in your memory.

And you will remember many a death and many days which went waste, a clock in the wall ticking your world to its end.

May your world prosper and you on your way home over the white streets like a man's mind, open with the edge of the knife, and boys standing in their quarrelsomeness studying nothingness: keenly they looked at you going without armour across a street burning at your feet, without armour but your harmonious spirit that never put a world in order but which will keep you, I hope, whole in your innocence like a coat.

THE OLD WOMAN

Tonight she is sitting by a window and the street like a bible below her eyes. The curtains have had many washings. There is a glitter from the flowered floor.

The world was once without shape, men and women like a red fever walking about flesh and mind, nostrils tasting love and anger.

Moon and sun in the sky, hand like salmon leaping to hand, the fish of the world in a net, pain that would not leave breast tranquil.

But everything has been set in order. Table in its place, chair in its place. This room is the mirror of her thoughts, arsenal from which will arise no music of growth.

For the music that will sing it together is youth itself that will never return. Her eye is sweeping the streets. Time is crouched in the window.

AT THE CEMETERY

I saw them yesterday at the cemetery, with black hats, and the sun rising, a glitter of flowers about their feet, and one wearing a bitter shirt.

Glitter of the sky, a sea singing, a pouring of grass, and a steadiness of mountains, the mortal conversation of dark hats, the poetry of summer upside down.

A wide day extending to the horizon. A bible burning in the hands of the wind and sun, and a sea falling like an empty dress on that shore.

And he is where he is. My neighbour lying under the bee which murmurs among sweet flowers. It was death that killed him and not a bullet.

And a sun pouring, a sea pouring, black hats darkly sailing on a sea of roses, as there move poor words on a tide of music.

AT THE STONES OF CALLANISH

At the stones of Callanish yesterday I heard one woman saying to another: 'This is where they burnt the children in early times.' I did not see druids among the planets nor sun nor robe: but I saw a beautiful blue ball like heaven cracking and children with skin hanging to them like the flag in which Nagasaki was sacrificed.

WHAT IS WRONG?

Who can tell what is wrong? I went to doctors and doctors. One of them told me, 'It's your head,' and another one, writing small with a pen, 'It's your heart, your heart.'

But one day I saw a black pit in green earth, a gardener kissing flowers, an old woman squeaking in her loneliness, and a house sailing on the water.

I don't know whether there is a language for that, or, if there is, whether I would be any better breaking my imagination into a thousand pieces: but one thing is certain, we must find the right that is wrong.

EIGHT SONGS FOR A NEW CEILIDH

(1)

You asked me for a poem for yourself, thinking, I suppose, that I would put you among the stars for beauty and intelligence.

But as for me I grew up in bare Lewis without tree or branch and for that reason my mind is harder than the foolish babble of the heavens, and also at Hiroshima the kettle boiled over our music and in Belsen there was seen an example of dishonour eating love and flesh, and because of that and because of the truth and all the Evil that was done to us, and we ourselves did (among our complaints) I will never put a pen again into my fist for beauty or for intellect. Beauty is dangerous enough and as for the mind did it not spoil the glittering cities of Europe?

But when one night I shall hear the quarrelsome beasts of love I will make a song for you that will illuminate the murder of the deer in the heather.

(2)

When she took the great sea on her, Lewis went away and will not
return. I was not compelled to sail 'over to Australia' but around me
is Hiroshima and Pasternak's book is in my hands—
    I will not drink a health-giving drink from the spring of the healthy
deer of May but from water full of eels which are electric and
shivering on my flesh like Venus breaking through the mind and the
dark-green of the clouds but it was the fine bareness of Lewis that
made the work of my mind like a loom full of the music of the
miracles and greatness of our time.

(3)

I saw myself in a camp among the Nazis and the wretched Jews. My
hand was white with the innocent lamps of Guernica and my cheek
streaming with piteous tears but in one hand there was a hard gun
while the gas was writhing like the mist of Lewis over cold rocks.

(4)

Standing at the end of the reservoir that was dumb, menacing, with
bare water, I saw the live flies hitting the dead flies on the back. The
foxglove was heavy about us with summer's perfume and the sky as
limpid as the music of a fiddle. In that moment you leaped and went
down, down into the water, and I was frightened that you wouldn't
rise and I shouted in spite of the skill of my intelligence but after that
I became silent.

(5)

I will not climb these mountains for what is at the top?
    The stars are holding a ceilidh but what can they say that is not in
my own dark depth? I will never sail on a ship. My Pacific is in my
head and my Columbus praising countries that are far below. The
day of my mind is my May and my twittering of birds the quick
thoughts that are black and yellow about my skies.

(6)

I will never go to France, my dear, my dear, though you are young. I
am tied to the Highlands. That is where I learnt my wound.
    And are we not tied to that as well? A door will open but where
will the slavish spirit of man go? I heard the wind blowing to the
Greeks at the Pillars of Hercules: our round world is more
harmonious than that. O, it is not a world of manliness that I am

speaking of but about the guilt that follows me from mountain and moor. My Uist is inside my head and my love like an agonising tether that is yellow and dangerous and beautiful.

(7)

'Go to London,' they said to me. 'In the great city you will compose music from the bitter hard light of your stomach.' And I was struggling with myself for many years, thinking of those streets, men with penetrating power in their faces, an illuminated glittering taxi flashing on the windows of my intelligence.

But tonight sitting at the fire and the hills between me and the sky and listening to the empty quietness and seeing the deer coming to my call I think of another one who said the truthful words: 'Look straight down through wood and wood. Look in your own heart and write.'

(8)

Will you go with me, young maiden, over to Japan where our sanity is wasting in that big bomb that fell on town and on mountain.

Not to Uist among the trees or to green Lewis among the heather nor a Farewell to Finnary burning calmly in the strait nor in the hall of Glasgow or Edinburgh and Duncan Ban walking elegantly with a bright gun among the lies that are clouds round our time.

OBAN

(1)

The rain is penetrating Oban and the circus has gone home. The lions and wildcats have gone home through the papers and advertisements. The seats are emptying at the mouth of the shore, in front of the houses in front of the pub—rain falling through the midst of the heavy salt of the sea.

(2)

Shall I raise a town of paper, with coloured lions on the wall, with great fierce tigers, and the wheel of music spinning?

Shall I raise a sky of paper? Clouds of paper, white lights?

Shall I make myself into paper, with my verses being cut on paper?

(3)

Tonight the sea is like an advertisement, book after book shining.
My shadow is running down to the sea. My skin is red and green.
Who wrote me? who is making a poetry of advertisements from
my bones? I will raise my blue fist to them.—'A stout Highlander
with his language.'

(4)

The circus has gone home. They have swept the sawdust away. The
pictures of beasts have gone. The rain is falling on the bay. The
wheel has gone off by itself. The season is over. The lion is running
through sunlight. He has left the rain behind his feet.

(5)

The big bell began to toll. The church has been opened. I sat down
inside it in my mind and saw on the window, instead of Nazareth and
Christ, worn earth and sawdust, a lion moving in the explosive circle
of Palestine without cease.

SIGHTING THE MOUNTAINS OF HARRIS

Sighting the mountains of Harris I saw neon on every street. An
Eventide behind the wall, and the gold sailors swimming on the
yellow sea of the cafés.

Advertisements on every hand. 'These are the mountains of
Harris, this is the end of my love.' Guitars glittering with light like
broken ships on the shore. Nylon girls in a doorway: the stones of
Woolworths in the bay.

Sighting the mountains of Harris, an armoury of light, a sea of
laughter and a green which is not the green of the sea swimming on
the face of a sailor.

THE SEA AND THE ROCKS

Ballet of foam against the rocks, these are my northern dancers. A
bare ignorant head that cannot understand the art of the tribe of
foolish dancers who leap and leap to a salt death: like pictures
thrown on a white screen, the hard beautiful lost ballet.

61

SONG OF REMEMBRANCE

Goodbye to Stornoway and the 'Muirneag' in the bay. The castle of our dream is glittering like a box full of Christmas.

O Stornoway and bare Lewis we need more iron than there is in these sails and that castle.

1941-42

Those days, on the radio, nothing but ships sinking in grey ignorant seas. I sat in the light of the Tilley listening to Big Ben tolling on the heavy eternal bottom of the sea.

THE MINISTER*

In the woods of Kintyre the minister began to squeak about the Amalekites and the Bible. Like a picture in the Old Testament the dew penetrating history, but his heart full of hatred and dryness. He ordered that the long swords should cut breast and skull, he wrote on them his Latin. A dry man of the silver buckles, black hose, was he not a bargain? God's servant and a devil of armies.

A high tide of blood about his shoes, wretched hands stretched out towards mercy, but he in the sun of happiness, and the dew falling, drop by drop, on the Amalekites beside him, like the murder of deer among the heather. And the crows from a blue space slanting to the rich manna among the trees and alighting on moustache or Bible.

*It is said that the Duke of Argyll's chaplain ordered that five hundred prisoners be put to death after they had surrendered. He did this because he was comparing them to the Amalekites and giving a warning that the same thing would happen as happened to Saul if they weren't killed.

THE RAIN

The rain pouring on the street. The rain pouring on my heart, on the lonely bridges of my heart, on the busy roads of my heart, the screen of red lights blazing about the blue cinemas of my heart.

SONG

I got up on a morning of May, and the radio playing loudly. I looked out on a window of shirts and the children shouting on the street. Radio Luxembourg blaring, O Young Girl of the Million Loves, ghost of nylon and ceilidhs swimming among the blue cookers.

LOVE SONG

'You left me and my mind was heavy,' your macintosh over your arm. I do not understand anything but this, the smell of your perfume: and your bones in the calm window of a supermarket.

THE HIGHLANDS

So much land, so much sea, this is a land for a poet who has lost his love for his fellow men. His pen is like a gull writing the screaming of loneliness.

LUSS

Roses swallowing the stone, a picture of a village instead of a true village. Beside the crouched cemetery there is one horse raising his old head out of time like an engraving of tranquil grey steel. And the children running among the graves and the sun. A picture of the roses of Scotland lying asleep in the picture of the windows which are heavy with heaven.

BARENESS

It is bareness I want, the bareness of the knife's blade. And the words to be going away from me like ducks settling on the sea when night is falling, their wings folded on the sea, and the night falling.

ON THE STREET

An old woman crying on the street. That is what I thought as I went past with my basket full of wine and bread—an apple, an orange, a banana, an old woman crying on the street, from world to world, under the Planet of the Old Woman.

INNOCENCE

The blue sea is like diamonds. O world, O world of innocence, how much destruction there is at the bottom of the sea, though your smile is so eternal—like God above and the Devil below.

THE ISLAND

There is an island always in the spirit so that we can flee there when the way is hard.

But they hit Malta from the sky in the ancient sea in the middle of the day. And Crete also suffered agony. Its guns were heard speaking. And Singapore was safe from the sea though it was broken from the north. And even on Lewis and Islay the aeroplanes of our time will burst, and angels and devils from the clouds descending through desperation or hope.

WHEN WE WERE YOUNG

When we were young it would be raining and we throwing stones at the telegraph poles unceasingly.

One horse would be standing against a wall, drenched by the rain, his skin slippery with the grey rain.

When we were young we would be playing football, with the moon in the sky like a football made of gold.

When we were young old women would be telling us, 'Don't do this, do that' for fear of the owl.

When we were young the sky would be empty, and pictures in the book, and the earth green and distant.

When we were young, there would be lies, when we are old the lie is that youth was without stain.

POEM

Liberal, Labour or Conservative, what business have they with us? The dark dry questions are breaking heads. And what have the red and blue to do with that dark river in which we swim, and the stars of Labour or Tories so dim among our oars?

MY POETRY

Well, I did not learn love from you. What I learnt was the truth. And without doubt the truth is hard as they will tirelessly tell us. But I remember a frosty night and the world open, south to north. O the sparkling sea was my choice. Who said that the truth is hard?

ONE GIRL

One girl I saw who was both intelligent and beautiful. That was two gifts from God. He opened his two fists over her.

I saw many who are intelligent and have learned many griefs. And also many a one has been seen who learned evil from beauty.

But truly the temptation will be sore when the two are together. For the world is full of thirst, and many, without either, pursuing them.

FREUD

Great man from Vienna who opened the mind with a knife keen with sore efficient happy light, and who saw the seas sweating with the blue-green ghosts of plague, and uncountable riches.

I follow the beasts with a joy that I cannot tell though I should be fishing from dungeon or from prison, as they move on that sea-bottom in the freedom of truth with their great helmets. No one will bring them to shore.

Cancer took your jaw away. But you were scanning with profundity the bottom of that sea where there are horrifying shadows. Father, mother and daughter fighting entwined together in a Greek play, in a strangling of forests.

The letter that I will not send, the letter that I will not keep, the poetry that my head cannot put together, the history that I would not want anyone to tell of my planets, the star is below in the seaweed of the skies.

Goodbye to the laughter of nature and the seas, goodbye to the salt that will bring tears to thoughts, goodbye to death which opens valuable countries, our rings are early in the weddings of our gifts.

O miracle of the waves and I tirelessly scrutinising you like a gay porpoise leaping in my country, it was you who gave us these new waves—your monument is on the bottom, and the seas are your pulpit.

THE WHITE SWAN*

The white swan is always there, even in the Great War, especially in the Great War, the white swan is swimming, on a river that they will never reach, those who die and those who return, at the far end of what happened to them, the white swan that will never die. With her long white neck, with her curiosity fishing among the canisters for clean water, where a house will be growing and the little children will be running, and the grey lark rising above distant chimneys.

*The White Swan is the title of a Gaelic love song about the First World War.

THE LITTLE OLD LADY

The little lady with the black hood, that snake among the heather, with her little sighs, O hi o ro, with her little sighs O hi o raobh, the little old lady of the communions, as clean as a diamond and on the side of God in the battle of sin, sniper of hell among the trees.

CONVERSATION

'You are old and I am young, let me go, let me go. Do you not see the rockets of our time? Do you not see Venus glittering?'

'Let me go, let me go, there are new birds in my heart. Will you not hear the young music? Will you not see Venus shining?'

'That was also what I said, "Let me go, let me go." But age and death are coming. And the dark sky is so far away. Goodbye then and may things go well with you. Venus is shining white. Age is withering her face like a little old lady with a little face.'

THE MELODEON OF THE SPIRIT

E hi o ro, e hi o ri, dance dance on the road, O melodeon of the spirit, dance dance at the end of the garden. O melodeon of the spirit, O distant hands faint and white in an autumn moon, O the active rash feet. O melodeon of the spirit, green and red and green again, there are ghosts at the end of the garden, our tears are falling.

There is a new music at the tips of our fingers, dance, dance on the road. O melodeon of my tears, the new music is shining over the ripening moon of the barley, the golden moon of the long night, the moon of boys, the moon of Lewis, the moon of the shoes of the new fashion.

PREDESTINATION

If I had done that, if I had done this, if I had read Calvin all day and into the small hours.

If I had attained my dream, if I had a million dollars, if it weren't for that long shadow that is always at my feet.

Calvin tells us that we are lost, Freud tells us that we are deceived. O my long thin hands why then are you writing?

And that great question in the shape of a snake moving on the lands of my father.

O my long thin hands, the world was lost when I was still a child.

And that long shadow in my bones from the very first day that I cried. Freud and Calvin come together like black angels and devils about my skies.

FOR DERICK THOMSON

(1)

We were brought up in Bayble together. There are many years since then. There were ghosts at the edge of the dyke and heather on Hol, and the stone round it. And an owl in the wave, and a wind shaking Mary Roderick, and the hen being blown to the moor. At the tips of our fingers was the dream. But the wind took low Bayble away. The boats are coming towards uncultivated soil and the terrifying corn. What is that cloud with the scowl?

What is that cloud on the Muirneag? What is that Bible opening and the leaves with wind and rain on them? What is the shadow that is troubling me? Whence is the thunder of the river? Who put these fish on the park? That eagle is high above my memory. Whence are these winds, Derick?

(2)

There is a tall mountain, the mountain of poetry, there is a tall mountain, the mountain of life. Which is the more difficult, which is the higher? The white ghosts are waiting.

Their large eyes are laughing, the helmets of Aignish catching us. O my guilts, O my shame, streets of names, row after row of them.

Above the mountain, mocking, is the sun of the spirit, waiting. Above Bayble, above the horizon, above the wells of life.

Above the great lights of the streets, above Homer, Aberdeen, above the white moon of my friends, above the crayon books.

67

Above the autumn of nuts, and that tall tree that is waiting. Like hens scattered across moorland, those Greeks who taught us life.

(3)

Bayble and Athens, isn't the compass strange and strict? How locked the lock is! There is a broken door in the glen.

Greek is on the broken door. There is a hawk on a chimney singing and saying: 'You are laid by. But I will open you to the chest.'

O beautiful hawk. O key of fire, teach me your beautiful poetry, your beak as innocent as a child's and as skilful as the work of intelligence.

(4)

In his beak he lifted Lewis and Bayble. In his beak he lifted me up. I saw Jupiter with its shadow steering heaviness over my sea.

And Mars and Venus going past, all the planets singing with the sweet choir of the thousand lights.

The Mod of the universe so sweet, bitter and sweet, that white choir, and the poet being crowned in the heavens, his face carved like a hawk's and his wings open, star on star.

(5)

The cuckoo is in the hawk's mouth. The chicken is in the crow's mouth. (The sore wind is in a great hurry.)

I will not put on my silken coat, my summer coat, in the bad weather and my fool's coat in pieces.

This century is throwing enough water at us like that great coloured tall bus that makes holes in the roads.

I will not leap from it, it is going too fast for me, it is putting the earth upside down. It is putting joy and hate on me, and my hair streaming to that wind, and my white face becoming a diamond against elegies and hymns, against the Iolaire and Holm, that song amongst the psalms, against the darkness and the blue and we now in our time with white lights, smooth lights on us, and Stornoway as small as a pin, but a golden hawk in that high sky like God, looking in a mirror.

68

THE PRODIGAL SON

Under the stars of grief, the thin glass in his hand, like ice which grows on pools, he listened to the dance. He listened to that music, the melodeon of his loss, he listened to his wounds in that golden distant country. His father running like a bird on tiptoe of joy, his brother breaking up the troublesome soil of dislike, the neighbours winking: 'What happened to you, dear? Wonderful the prosperity that has come on the little boy of our song.'

What sort of place were you in? Is it beautiful, is it new? Is it wine that is in the well, whisky instead of water? Is there reaping without labour, is the autumn to your wish? Will corn be found in the barn on the great morning of the dew?

And the dance goes past, the dance of the planets and the people. He looked down inside the glass that was foolish and thin. He saw the stony eyes and he was filled with a sort of shivering and he sat there like a kettle on the dishonourable fire of the world.

And he heard the thunder of feet, the dance of past fashions. He felt again the rainstorms that spoilt the seasons before his step. He felt again the locks, the dangerous prison of lies. 'O God, who put this spark in my breast in vain,' he shouted in the unsteady winter and he threw the glass from his hand.

It turned over beneath the moon. It broke on the uncultivated soil. He got up and went home: 'This place is as good as others,' he shouted through the untellable music and the planets of a million laughters.

THE POPPY

The flower of Flanders is red in the blue sky. That blood is still strong amidst the storm.

That red star is on my calm jacket. The hands are folded and the eyes are shut.

The potatoes are growing and the roots are so white, the dead bones among the water and the dew.

And the cows with their helmets and their great horns tasting grass that was cleansed by them and each skull quiet under the plough gently fertilising the earth far from heaven.

SATURDAY

Here on Saturday evening, nothing but a dark tiredness in my soul, nothing but a blanket on my eyes or the two Greek coins, nothing but a seagull going past the narrow window of the stone, nothing but an earth that has gone waste on us and left me with this tiredness.

For the soul needs blossom as the potato does, the soul needs a thistle woven in peace and turmoil, it needs renewing and restlessness, it needs more than the graves that I see at that stone church with those long narrow windows, with the steeple that is rising to an empty sky that is in pieces with black heavy slow clouds, the rainy bare sky of sheep, sky of cows, sky of that weariness, sky of the moon as she rises from the poor broken bodies of the heavens, a broken woman in her nightgown seeking a world that has gone astray on her.

DEIRDRE

O Glen Etive, O Glen Etive, Deirdre made her way over the sea. The whistle of Naoise took her to Ireland, the beautiful girl of our songs and instead of berries her eyes rested on the red blood of the wrong spring. The dagger descended through the room like a beaked seagull into the sea.

O Glen Etive, O Glen Etive, you did not save her when she left the innocent hollow of lies and followed the whistling of death.

THE HEROES

There are some whom death will not break though the graip goes through them: and a man will eat cut potatoes, for that wound is simple.

I prefer them to whole potatoes with their faces full of hope, so stolid and foolish and so white on the plate of bad sweetness.

AUTUMN SONG

They have taken the corn in, they have folded up the mountains. The moon is in the back room on an old prudent sideboard. You are sleeping in your autumn and I in my mind am walking street after street, my talent beside me.

O sleep easily and quietly, sleep without turning and do not listen at night to my feet wakeful in your world.

THE FOOL

In the dress of the fool, the two colours that have tormented me—English and Gaelic, black and red, the court of injustice, the reason for my anger, and that fine rain from the mountains and these grievous storms from my mind streaming the two colours together so that I will go with poor sight in the one colour that is so odd that the King himself will not understand my conversation.

TO MY MOTHER

You were gutting herring in distant Yarmouth and the salt sun in the morning rising out of the sea, the blood on the edge of your knife, and that salt so coarse that it stopped you from speaking and made your lips bitter.

I was in Aberdeen sucking new courses, my Gaelic in a book and my Latin at the tiller, sitting there on a chair with my coffee beside me and leaves shaking the sails of scholarship and my intelligence.

Guilt is tormenting me because of what happened and how things are. I would not like to be getting up in the darkness of the day gutting and tearing the fish of the morning on the shore and that savage sea to be roaring down my gloves without cease.

Though I do that in my poetry it is my own blood that is on my hands, and every herring that the high tide gave me palpitating till I make a song, and instead of a cooper my language always hard and strict on me, and the coarse salt on my ring bringing animation to death.

THE OLD WOMAN

The postman will come tonight with the Christmas letter. The postman will come tonight with light on his clothes. Does anyone know what will be in the letter? 'The sharp star of the Bible,' said the old woman who was waiting alone in a dream.

ON A BEAUTIFUL DAY

From the stone the wildcat is watching the world. The hare shakes like a lily. The hawk and the lark are in the same mirror and the sun shining and the grass growing. The wildcat is drinking champagne

71

over his teeth. The hare is halted, listening with ears like doors. The hawk is sitting on its wings drinking the wind, and the lark singing like a record in a Gaelic cloud.

THE STONE

I will tell you, my dear, the words that the stone told me. The stone has never heard of Lewis or about songs. The stone is a prisoner under the lightning. The lightning is weaving a light around the stone like an old woman who has gone mad.

The stone is inside the prison thinking about darkness, about clouds, about shells, and about other stones.

But at the end it is thinking of itself alone.

And because of that and because of poetry which is weaving a swift light about the stone, this is what the stone said to me on a winter's night or a summer's night far from the moon and the restless sea that will not find sleep again but is walking the world at three o'clock in the morning.

This is what the stone told me: 'I am waiting. The longest river will reach its end. The brightest spirit will reach its conclusion. And at the end of the matter I will rise in front of it and in the middle of the thunder I will be like a king.'

RAVEN

Writing the last words I gave my pen to a raven. 'What have you to say to them? What story is in your heart?'

He looked at me with cold eyes. He put ice on my sight. And then he wrote with permanence: 'Tell them that I will be paying a visit.'

'But our music,' I said to him. 'Our poetry, book after book. O miracle of the northern lights, the imagination of Dante and Homer.'

'I know,' I shouted to him, 'the Odyssey of greatness. They kept you in mind but swallowed you with hope.'

And he threw down the pen. The window was hard with marvellous and strict light and the raven lost in my comfort.

IV

THREE POEMS FOR CHRISTMAS

I

The dark begins to close in.
The November dark.
What stirs beneath the ground?
What is readying?

No growth without pain.
That is the hard lesson.
No lolloping hare without
the weasel's tooth.

Weasels quiver like the northern lights.
Ounces of pure hate
they loosen the rats' teeth from small bones
inside the murderous green.

The November dark falls.
The shop windows have flat even light.
Dummies smile in their cages
with bright unfocussed eyes.

Soon it will be Christmas.
The body is sold again,
beautiful as the lily
the colour of beaten copper.

II

Now the radiator fumes in the lobby.
How desperately cold it is!
Lorries are slewed across roads
on a wicked ice. And the high sky
is humming an electric blue.

In boyhood how we tasted flakes.
Sleigh-bells and an attic window
peering like an eye out of the snow
that surged up in beautiful blind waves
like Santa Claus's beard.

We get soft, that's it.
The back assumes the armchair's shape.
We turn from the news to the Third Programme.
A talk on Ravel is preferable
to the coils of Vietnam.

To have felt everything so intensely
is like skin after skin peeling off.
The cold is more piercing after
these gifts of youth which through a sensitive skin
exploded and now fall.

III

In the terrible white of the light I hear ticking.
The silver Christmas bells have a slanting song.
In drunken flashes what a tree we've climbed,
from the slime below this house to its calm study.

In the stunning sea and earth the radiant fish
and equally radiant animals kill each other.
Superb assurance presses on the nerve
of the bell's effrontery where the ravens circle.

The rats gnaw our atlases. Seagulls plunge
into the orbs of Homer. The pale lily
shakes where the cruising eel and cannibal trout
feed in deep lochs, the million years below us.

The Christmas Card in Vietnam is bordered
with Joy, Great Joy, another hundred killed.
The mind, appraised on crooked bearings, is
a jagged star zooming in to kill.

The rats ascend by waste. By waste we climb
this flashing tree with all its silver worlds.
The bells ring out their hollow cool perfection.
This tree is fiercely calmed by our fierce hands.

WHY ARE YOU?

Why are you always going to the library?
There is nothing there.
You take out books like mirrors.

Better to sink without trace
in the place where the storms aren't yours
where the lightnings are foreign

than to move from volume to volume
seeing in each new title
the groove that will not be filled!

I BUILD AN ORANGE CHURCH

I build an orange church and put inside it
a little orange minister in a pulpit
that's dandelion yellow.

I make a ceiling of intensest blue.
The seats are heliotrope, the bibles pink,
hymn books are apple green.

Picasso paints the walls with animals.
The angels swoop in red and there's a sun
of blinding nuclear light.

And so transform it all. . . . But for the guilt
that's small and black and creeps in when the door
swings on its oiled hinges.

WHAT'S YOUR SUCCESS?

What's your Success to me who read the great dead,
whose marble faces, consistent overhead,

outstare my verse? What are your chains to me,
your baubles and your rings? That scrutiny

turns on me always. Over terraced houses
these satellites rotate and in deep spaces

the hammered poetry of Dante turns
light as a wristwatch, bright as a thousand suns.

THOSE WHO ACT

Those who act,

who bring the rope at the right time,

who know the kiss of life, have learnt
where the syringes and the drugs are,

Those who grow in the fact,

who see the stone in its perfect shadow
and do not ask why yellow is yellow,

To whom the car whirling in gravel
is that itself: and the will
itself, itself;

let these in their place be honoured
where the visible earth hangs on the cord

they pull: and light comes on.

AND THIS IS HELL

'And this is hell,
nor am I out of it'
where the vases harden
and take on shape
long-lasting, with fine pictures.

Heaven above the ceiling is too easy.
The clouds drift
over the pale hand
without cunning
(yellowing in the yellowy daffodil light).

Where the smoke swirls
and the stink of straw
refines the nostrils
and the devil's
handsome face smiles
is where the vase collects
itself, becomes a cup
handed over smiling
by a Satan leaning
into the cheers of Prize Day.

POEM

Some move others but themselves are stone.
Present them honour? No, present them none.
An alert coldness is to be despised
or let us praise the viper, the owl's eyes
globular in darkness, or the snow
that drifts forever on the world below.
Better the headlong soldier in his wrath
than the cool hand that plotted his hot graph,
O better in our vain and passionate wars
Love that moves the sun and the other stars.

HAMLET

Sick of the place, he turned him towards night.
The mirrors flashed distorted images
of himself in court dress, with big bulbous eyes,
and curtains swaying in a greenish light.

Save me from these, he cried, I could not kill.
I did not have the true and pure belief
even to marry, reproduce myself
in finite mirrors, tall and visible.

Bad jokes and speeches, I endured them all,
so therefore let my death be a bad joke.
I see in the warped mirrors rapiers shake
their subtle poisons perfuming the hall

reflecting accidents, a circus merely,
a place of mirrors, an absurd conclusion.
Images bounce madly against reason
as, in a spoon, wide pictures, fat and jolly.

I could not kill, but let them have their deaths
imprisoned in this air in which they perish
where only lies and ponderous jokes can flourish.

Remove the mirror, for there is no breath.

79

HEAR US O LORD

Hear us, O Lord, aggression is part of us.
You polish your jewellery in the salons of heaven.
Everything about you glitters, your wrist-watch, the diamond
at your invisible breast, below your invisible beard.

We are such ferocious animals, Lord, we're irrational.
The long journey of the lizard was propelled by this
to the green Jaguar standing in the driveway.
As you polish your nails we begin to hate you.

All those who tell us the truth we hate.
All those who were strong—like Hitler and Stalin—we loved.
We are obsessed by the table with the green light on it.
We practise with knives in the boudoir and the church.

Ah, if it were only a game. But all things happen.
Because we have spoken too much a heaven has fallen.
Because we have loved too much a door has been slammed.
We stare at the light of Envy green in the night.

What should we do to be saved? The screen slowly brightens.
You watch us with interest, a glass of pale wine in your hand.
'The things that they do, the plays that my actors perform.'
We keep you alive in the silence, in an absence of angels.

GLASGOW

City, cauldron of a shapeless fire,
bubbling with brash Irish and a future

that stares from fifteen stories towards the Clyde.
The cotton and tobacco plants have died

Plantation St. is withered. You love your ships,
hate your police, in whisky-coloured sleeps

adore your footballers. Victoria's not amused
at Celtic Park or Ibrox where the horsed

dice-capped policemen, seared by pure flame
trot in white gauntlets round your serious game

and the roaring furnaces bank your last pride.
They shed the rotting tenements flying goalward.

THE HOUSE WE LIVED IN

The house we lived in for five years
in slummy Dumbarton
was almost falling down.
Everything had a padlock and chain.

Above us were fights each night.
Chairs broken like matches
and the wife sporting a black eye.
'I slipped'—defiantly.

Every Friday night
her husband would doll himself
by the one rayed mirror
in his suit sharp as a razor.

Every Friday night
he'd be beaten up
by swarming Catholics
for cursing the good Pope

robed in his Vatican
under the Italian blue
and far from the hubbub
of that fierce provincial pub.

Every Saturday morning
her blacked eye would shine
like a new sin
in her unvanquished face.

Scrubbing the marble cinema steps . . .
her husband strolling by
unemployed and spry
wearing his blue suit

with the blood scrubbed away.
Nothing green, I remember,
but for the innocent eyes
calm and murderous.

RETURN TO THE COUNCIL HOUSE

Box on box, on ledge after ledge rising
I used at midnight to come home
to your uniform sparkle on a bare hill,
my Rome of the clamped mussels.

O Rome, city of the wolves,
in what office did a man sit
among diminished clarities
designing you with a rigid appetite?

Under crown after crown of neon light
I approached you, the Yale in my hand,
as to an alien island
whirling in the blue sky of TV

and the wife hoarding her plot
her little handkerchief of green,
where the mower lay on its side
and she had her day for the washing.

From the scarred bus shelter I climbed
to my Rome of fixed lines.
The pad of the wolves is tense
among the chequered shadows,

the drift of figures in the blue caves,
the writing on the wall,
the stone steps in their spiral,
from room to room the same.

AT THE HIGHLAND GAMES

Like re-reading a book which has lost its pith.

Watching the piper dandying over a sodden stage
saluting an empty tent.

The empty beer glasses catch the sun
sparkle like old brooches against green.

Fur-hatted, with his huge twirling silver stick
the pipe-major has gypsy cheekbones, colour of brick.

Everything drowses. The stewards with aloof eagle stare
sit on collapsing rock, chair on brown chair.

Once the pibroch showed the grave 'ground'
of seas without bubbles, where great hulks were drowned,

meat with moustaches. The heroic dead die
over and over the sea to misty Skye.

Past the phantom ivy, bird song, I walk
among crew-cuts, cameras, the heather-covered rock,

past my ancestry, peasant, men who bowed
with stony necks to the daughter-stealing lord.

Past my ancestry, the old songs, the pibroch
stirring my consciousness like the breeze a loch.

Past my buried heart my friend who complains
of 'All the crime, their insane violence.'

Stone by stone the castles crumble. The seas
have stored away their great elegies.

'Morag of Dunvegan.' Dandy piper
with delicate soft paws, knee-bending stepper,

saluting an empty tent. Blue-kilted stewards
strut like strange storks along the sodden sward.

Finished. All of it's finished. The Gaelic
boils in my mouth, the South Sea silver stick

twirls, settles. The mannequins are here.
Calum, how you'd talk of their glassy stare,

their loud public voices. Stained pictures
of what was raw, violent, alive and coarse.

I watch their heirs, Caligulas with canes
stalk in their rainbow kilts towards the dance.

SCHOOL SPORTS, AT THE TURNSTILES

This is impossible. Though I know
(and have been told) the world's absurdity
(a dewdrop poised on nothing,
a zero
containing continually our comic seething)

and though all day wearily I've watched the flags
droop a little lower and heard money
clink at the long strides of young runners
negotiating curves in the uninteresting
way sports have, of having no ceasing,

yet suddenly I cheered as in the twilight
over the soaking ground the last came running
stretching for a prize they might not have
for more than a moment, as if somehow coming home
could be like this, a proud and hopeful yearning.

MR M.

O how Mr M's Latin gown
frothed after him like a boat in water.

Raised on grammar, he flushed from these woods
not pheasants but Aeneas and the rest

dressed in the supine and infinitive
ghosts of words, ghosts of innocence, language
beautiful, tough, persistent.

Caesar and the ablative absolute together
harrying barbarous tribes.
The Roman roads undeviating as
an arrow or a sword.

And the wooden desks cut with knives.
Names of children deep in knotted fields
buried like Roman legions.

These fought their own battles
in the lavatories of weeping stone.
Under the taps, inverted heads
sucked at their cold fountains.

And today the holiday planes
ferry them to Italy
on cheap excursions to effeminate
wine and flowering music.

O that school where we were young,
the order's broken. We visit its old stones,
dishonoured consuls visiting Hades
(green field and ponderous doors)

but there are only ghosts there now.
We clutch your ghostly gown like Orpheus
clutching at Eurydice while Pluto
giggles on iron coins.

IN THE CLASSICS ROOM

In summer how lovely the girls are
even here where Vergil is king of the walk,

where the hooded owl eyes have brooded all winter
on a text, a lacuna, a gap in a line
where the power is undischarged

and the dusty bulbs swung metrically in a draught
blowing in from the Western Sea.

How easy it was to forget them, the girls,
how easy to believe they were only dresses,
satchels, hollow heads to be filled with poetry.

Now it is they themselves who fill with poetry
brimming each day with more and more of their wine.

O Dido, in your pillar of fire
excessively burning in Carthage,
who is this Aeneas whose wood has grown subtle

who is this Roman whose glasses reflect your fire
whose legs twitch uncontrollably like an infant's
whose book shakes like a leaf?

FOR L.

Practical girl, worker of cloth and of silver,
maker of jewellery, sets for an amateur stage,
I think, as I hear, of my own obsessional talent
thin as a needle, wandering, swift as an elver,
and my pride declines in the light of your various moon.

To move with such grace from one light to another
is closer to life, Naera. So would I rather,
in your serious clasp, grasp also your various talent,
learn from your manifold scope, your changeable weather,
Persephone's arts, the seasons of furious change

and you from my single progression the current that charges
the movement of various waters, the tall elm that anchors
leaves to their amorous shadows in excess of play
the strength of the thigh to the muscles' beautiful surges—
the single and multifarious, married and free.

THE DEPARTING ISLAND

Strange to see it—how as we lean over
this vague rail, the island goes away
into its loved light grown suddenly foreign:
how the ship slides outward like a cold ray
from a sun turned cloudy, and rough land draws down
into an abstract sea its arranged star.

Strange how it's like a dream when two waves past,
and the engine's hum puts villages out of mind
or shakes them together in a waving fashion.
The lights stream northward down a wolfish wind.
A pacing passenger wears the air of one
whom tender arms and fleshly hands embraced.

It's the island that goes away, not we who leave it.
Like an unbearable thought it sinks beyond
assiduous reasoning light and wringing hands,
or, as a flower roots deep into the ground,
it works its darkness into the gay winds
that blow about us in a later spirit.

87

TO HAVE FOUND ONE'S COUNTRY

To have found one's country
after a long journey
and it to be here
around one all the time.
It is like taking a girl
from the house next door,
after all that travel
that black dense wall.

To have fallen in love with
stone, thistle and strath,
to see the blood flow
in wandering old rivers,
this wound is not stanched
by handkerchiefs or verse.
This wound was after all
love and a deep curse.

Now I'm frightened to name it
lest some witch should spring
screaming out of the tombs
with a perverted broom.
I'm almost frightened to
name all the waters,
these seas, tall hills,
these misty bordered bibles.

Love's such a transient thing
except for that hard slogging
which, though it's love, we don't
name it by that ring
in which, tortured, we fight
with all the bones about us
in these cemeteries that hold
the feet in living grass.

THE HALL

The hall is large and echoing. You are small.
Speech after speech. I will not tell you all

my heart is thinking of. You say, 'The rates
are far too high.' And then, 'Suggested sites

for the new hall are really quite absurd.'
Speech after speech. The nightingales once heard

Socratic dialogues but did not know
the place was a loved prison. And the slow

poison beat its oars out on Death's stream.
I might have asked a question if the dream

had not so held me of the rooted state
the weight of leaves, the tentacles of light,

that where we love we stay in spite of all
and why we love, no burrowing mind can tell.

DUNCAN BAN MACINTYRE

This Gaelic bard fell in love with a small corrie.
Patiently he numbered each blade of grass
with an attentiveness akin to fury
or Celtic monk carving a Celtic cross
with such an intent delicacy, such precision,
that love itself made visionary what was
merely a little corrie. Without passion
it would have remained what now it no longer is.

Now it's more than a corrie. Genius made it
a book, a poem, a place to be wondered at.
Strange deer move in it. It is green-shaded
with a peculiar unalterable light.
A remarkable place soaked in the spirit of one
who was gentle happy tranquil and a careful
meticulous poet who loved every stone
and every slope, and who was always cheerful.

Who knew the way the sun settled just there
at a certain time of the day and how that shadow
seemed to vibrate in the evening air.
And the deer grazed like cattle in a meadow.
How the hinds and delicate fawns are shy and fearful
and run like pure wind among the shadows and stones,
drinking the air with delicate nostrils. How tearful
on the other hand they die in the sound of guns.

All poetry's made by love and his life shows it.
An ordinary man unable to read or write,
this corrie in Argyllshire made him a poet.
Whatever it was that made that glen all light
worked in his heart till speech was necessary.
Natural as a lark he sang his song
and patient too as a scientist who would marry
music to fact, research to a musical tongue.

HOMAGE TO
GEORGE ORWELL

(1)

You knew well in advance
of the rest of us what's true—
that you can't look at a rose
without seeing a Fascist
with his closed red fist.
That the hazy hills
around us every day
are the hills of Spain
where the dry olives
patter into graves.
That 'concentration' means,
among other things,
concentration camps.
And that over the leaves
of your loose notebook
not the light of the lamp
only, but the two

yellow eyes of the sick
Deutschland, the paranoic
warmly-feathered gauleiter,
burning brighter and brighter
nightly on your cottage
implacably perpend.

(2)

In my little house
on a distant island
I used to scribble poems
on an oil-skinned table.
But I didn't know
what I've learnt to know—
what inhuman pressures
keep a line of verse
on its own course.
How a cult of slaves
kept in their fixed place
the elaborated lines
of a Greek vase.

(3)

Lorca falls
with the poem in front of his face
riddled with holes.
Cloaks like playing cards
turn away
across Spain,
a green piece
in a jigsaw.
He falls
deep in the scarred earth
a lift plunging.
Now he rises.
Inside the golden box
he plays his proud guitar.

(4)

The pack surround him,
Jacks, kings and queens.
Spades dig in the green

earth. Clubs
fall out of the air.
Hearts turn small, fear
makes the bright diamonds shrink.
The pack falls
on a green table
under green hands.

His face, part shade, part light,
holds its hauteur
carving the future
like a prow.
Outside,
the gipsy music invigorates his mask.
Rectangular cloaks retain
pistols and holsters.
Under a yellow moon
bodies put off their gear,
are fish in the silver pools,
are silver reeds,
are gipsies
telling his fortune.

(5)

Lorca goes marching underground
with his phosphorescent guitar.
He strolls into a bar
and the peasants gather round.

His breast is full of holes
and all that music
sets his white shirt dancing
just like so many souls

all divided, all united,
by the bullet holes.

JEAN BRODIE'S CHILDREN

Jean Brodie's children in your small green caps,
I hear you twitter down the avenues.

The great round bells ring out, the Mademoiselle
despairs of English. In the rustling dorms
you giggle under sheets.

'Dear Edinburgh, how I remember you,
your winter cakes and tea, your bright red fire,
your swirling cloaks and clouds.

Your grammar and your Greek, the hush of leaves,
No Orchids for Miss Blandish with a torch
beneath the tweedy blanket.

Ah, those beautiful days, all green and shady,
our black and pleated skirts, our woollen stockings,
our ties of a calm mauve.

Mistresses, iron in their certainty,
their language unambiguous but their lives
trembling on grey boughs.'

SHE TEACHES LEAR

Much to have given up? Martyr, one says?
And to read *Lear* to these condemning ones
in their striped scarves and ties but in the heart
tall, cool and definite. Naval, in this art.
'Brought it on himself. He ran away,
then strained to keep his pomp and circumstance.'

Of course it's true. Much to be said for Regan,
Goneril too. Cordelia just a tune,
and also beautiful as I am not.

'Life must be lived. Life is beyond thought.
These two were living.' Who says that? It's Brown.
The smallest one (with glasses) in the room.

So I go home towards his bitterness,
achieved selfishness, clinging so with claws
to chair and pipe, a dreadful bitter man.
He hates all life, yet lives. Helpless in pain,
trains pain on others. 'Pray,' at night he says,
'undo this button,' and yet hates for this

me out of helplessness. And yet I stay.
'Regan and Goneril had some place to go.'
('Somewhere.' Correct this young American.)
Which side is right? For there is young pale Jean—
she might be one. Responsibility
is weighty, living, in the to-and-fro

of these cool deadly judgments. So she listens,
the true Cordelia, library-white face,
thin-boned and spectacled, speechlessly unhappy,
and ready for all art, especially poetry.
'They had some place to go and pure passions.
The rest's hypocrisy.' Purity of the race?

No, not as far as that, Simply a lie,
to live and feed with one so selfish grown
as age is always selfish. The proud two
spur their tall horses into the bright blue
in search of lust, are willing so to die,
the absolute hunters, Goneril and Regan,

beautiful too with their own spare beauty
when one forgets the haunted piteous fox
(there's always a fox whenever such ride by).
Does Jean, as I do, sniff it? Memory
of dear addictive fences, of the high
tall splendid brutes, past little dreaming flocks.

And yet . . . More simply. They are what they are,
I am what I am? The sensitive eye
broods by packed windows of interior pain
fastened to writhings, knowing rages mean
often unhappiness, that old men wear
their stubborn angers out of dignity,

the failing vigour—eyes, arms, knees.
Gravity pulls them down into the ground.
Last anger blossoms on its final lip.
'Lear is a child,' I hear. Is this the deep
Greek brilliant irony? I find my peace
in this dictator because I have no kind

child to nourish. No, it's not quite that.
'We'll come to this,' I cry. 'No,' Moira says,
quite definite and calm. 'If I should come
to such a state let all drive me from home.'
Easy enough, I think (but hold the thought)
to speak such words when interested praise

makes your face happy at the Saturday
school-club dance, in yellow, and a hand
glides down your bare arm, it seems, forever.
Why should I speak, this loud, my own fever?
And then I know it's right as far's mind may
(without sly falsity) seek to understand.

'It's just in case,' I say, 'in case, malformed'—
(how vulnerable ties and scarves, how pure!)
'by living we are made. It's just in case'—
the need, the need!—Polite and curious
they know of no such need (but Jean). Not armed
nor yet disarmed they sit. Sure or unsure

it hasn't touched them yet, the fear of age.
Regan and Goneril seem more natural.
From our own weakness only are we kind.
Admire such ones but know in your own mind
how they would bring upon us innocent carnage,
the end of Lear, and *Lear*, their own worse will.

ENTERING YOUR HOUSE

Entering your house, I sniff again
the Free Church air, the pictures on the wall
of ministers in collars, all these dull
acres of brown paint, the chairs half seen
in dim sad corners by the sacred hall

under the spread antlers of that head
mildly gazing above leathern tomes.
So many draperies in so many rooms.
So many coverlets on each heavy bed.
A stagnant green perpetuates these glooms.

And then the stairs. The ancient lamps and the
scent of old prayers, texts of 'God is Love.'
Did any children grow through all this grief?
The ceilings seem to sigh, the floor to be
carpeted by a threadbare dim belief.

Such pressures on the head. And then I see
in an oval frame an eighteen-year-old girl
like Emily Bronte staring from the peril
of commandments breaking round her. And I pray
that she was happy, curl on winding curl,

even though I see the stains around her face,
the ancient tints of brown that eat at brow
and hair and nose, and make me see her now
as almost rusted in this world of grace.
How little beauty conscious sins allow!

I enter the great garden with its red
and dripping roses, laburnums and the tall
tulips and the columbines, the small
and holy Rose of Sharon. All the dead
are lost in colour as the dewdrops fall.

I watch a bee nuzzling from tower to tower
of brilliant yellow, each with soundless bell,
its hairy body busy in the smell
and light of evening. From flower to flower
it flies and sucks, quivers, then is still,

so gross and purposeful I can forget
the tall and simple flowers it feeds on here
in this bright garden of a freer air.
I pray that she, some gross and fruitful night,
under less heavy coverlets as bare

as these tall flowers, allowed new life to start
from her body's honey, turning to the wall
that portrait of her father, stern and tall.
And that the Rose of Sharon at her heart
quivered and quietened in her radiant fall.

AT THE SALE

Old beds, old chairs, old mattresses, old books.
old pictures of coiffed women, hatted men,
ministers with clamped lips and flowing beards,
a Duke in his Highland den,
and, scattered among these, old copper fire-guards,
stone water-bottles, stoves and shepherds' crooks.

How much goes out of fashion and how soon!
The double-columned leather-covered tomes
recall those praying Covenanters still
adamant against Rome's
adamant empire. Every article
is soaked in time and dust and sweat and rust. What tune

warbled from that phonograph? Who played
that gap-toothed dumb piano? Who once moved
with that white chamber pot through an ancient room?
And who was it that loved
to see her own reflection in the gloom
of that webbed mirror? And who was it that prayed

holding that Bible in her fading hands?
The auctioneer's quick eyes swoop on a glance,
a half-seen movement. In the inner ring
a boy in serious stance
holds up a fan, a piece of curtaining,
an hour-glass with its trickle of old sand.

We walk around and find an old machine.
On one side pump, on another turn a wheel.
But nothing happens. What's this object for?
Imagine how we will
endlessly pump and turn for forty years
and then receive a pension, smart and clean,

climbing a dais to such loud applause
as shakes the hall for toiling without fail
at this strange nameless gadget, pumping, turning,
each day oiling the wheel
with zeal and eagerness and freshness burning
in a happy country of anonymous laws,

while the ghostly hands are clapping and the chairs
grow older as we look, the pictures fade,
the stone is changed to rubber, and the wheel
elaborates its rayed
brilliance and complexity and we feel
the spade become a scoop, cropping the grass,

and the flesh itself becomes unnecessary.
O hold me, love, in this appalling place.
Let your hand stay me by this mattress here
and this tall ruined glass,
by this dismembered radio, this queer
machine that waits and has no history.

OLD WOMAN WITH FLOWERS

These are your flowers. They were given to you
so nurse them carefully and tenderly.
Though flowers grow freely elsewhere, here in this room
there's not much space, so therefore like a child
let no one else go near them.
                    O dear God
wherever you are, I am almost driven wild
by your frightening flowers whose blossoms are turned to bone
for an old woman to look at, in a small room alone.

OLD WOMAN

Overwhelmed with kindnesses—and you have nothing.
They bring you roses to refresh their hearts
and still the bitter voices.

They greet you sweetly, you are now their child,
they flatter you completely,
and you have nothing to present to them
objects to objects, just your used self.

Only a god I think could take such gifts
and not feel hatred. Only a god could bear
such manifold penances, and be the vase
for all these guilty roses.

You are no god and therefore should you snap
suddenly out at them between old teeth
like a fox dying in a sweet country
I should not turn from that poor twisted face
bayed in its autumn by solicitous smiles.

IN OLD AGE

Now you sleep away the day which has nothing to offer.
Let it keep its roses, ruins and stones, its rivers and mountains.
Its streets have gone away to another country
where lanes may lead in mist to incredible encounters.
Loaves, apples, oranges, guardsmen, statues have been packed away
for ever behind the eyes. Nothing now can come of them.
You have shut your eyes like the blue shutters of cafés
and not even the last green slit of sunset can be seen.
The newspapers have written their last scandal, the novels are ended.
For you there is only the fire and the sleep of exclusion.
Though at two a.m. a hundred worms dance on the lawn.

IF YOU ARE ABOUT TO DIE NOW

If you are about to die now
there is nothing I can write for you.
History is silent about this.
Even Napoleon, face huge as a plate,
disguised the advance guard and said:
'Why they sent for my brother is because
he, and not I, is in trouble.'

The screens come down. The nurses disappear
like the tails of fishes. The clouds
are white as cotton wool and also
Dettol outlives the perfume.
The unshaven man in the next ward
is given Shaving Lotion for Christmas.
Sorrow stands like a stork on one leg,
brooding.

The coloured windows give way to plain.
The horsemen crossing the moor are comrades
going the other way into the country
of the undisciplined and the free.
Here there is the Land of the Straight Lines
with a banner black and silent,
a black mirror
with the image of an old rose.

History does not warn us of this.
Napoleon's face expands to a window.
The manic thoughts fly outwards, beating.
'The documents did not tell me.
There was no announcement in the salon.
Why is it that the chairs are getting crooked?
Why is it that my army does not hear me?
They are eating, laughing by the stream.

I shout to them, "Put on your armour."
But they do not listen.
They do not know me, they are relapsing
into the marsh of their idleness.
They are schoolboys escaped from Latin.
O how afraid they are of Excellence.
They admire their faces in the water.

They splash in the new bubbles.'

V

from LIGHT TO LIGHT

So many lights.
Lights on a bay,
an old churchyard,
where the tombs lean
like old men in conversation,
light falling on trees
(as out at Gallanach
facing the Atlantic
the trees stand like barometers
the sap rising in them).
This is in early spring
but in summer
they're luxuriant in leaves
and the rooks caw round the fissures
of old, immensely old, rocks
in their love-play
circling.
The light on Coire Cheathaich
Where Duncan Ban Macintyre, our Gaelic poet,
created from an ordinary place
a place of genius,
Macintyre our illiterate bard
unable to read or write
who saw the deer moving waxen-skinned
in a light that is not our light,
the light of love.
That equable happy and cheerful man
who shot the deer with poetry.
My eye sweeps now
over name after name,
Dalmally, Lochgilphead, Benderloch,
Mull, Tobermory,
'the well of the Virgin Mary,'
Inverary,
Campbeltown,
black Glencoe 'where the deer starve for the rifle,'

many castles,
many churchyards,
many hills.
Here in Argyllshire Scotland was begun
where the green light was nourished
by monks in their careful cells
their illuminated manuscripts.

And where the light may end
or blaze in a dazzle of blue
as once over Hiroshima,
Nagasaki,
the Japanese looked up and saw
a ball of bright blue fire
so dazzling, so pure, so lovely,
like a child's celestial balloon,
they didn't know it was death
and where once there was a man
standing by a wall casually
there was only a shadow,
a clear-cut silhouette.
For, as my eye traverses
in affection and fear this county,
I begin again from the west bay of Dunoon
where visitors stand by railings
looking out towards America
and the moon hangs in the sky
like a silver dollar
(high above the pink decorative lights
which string the foreshore)
and crammed in taxis the American sailors
set out 'to see the town.'
My eye moves from that statue
of Highland Mary (O Burns
will you survive
our high-powered dose of hydrogen
stronger than any whisky you drank)
towards Sandbank and its yachts
and towards the Holy Loch
where our American ships
guard that civilisation
which goes on and off like a Belisha beacon,
precarious, delicate.

From Iona to the Holy Loch,
from green to blue,
from the dosage of religion
nourished among gardens and shadows,
from a man with a white horse,
a great and bridled poet,
a man with a dove's name
who yet had a hawk's head.
From the small coracle
to the great ships,
from the seed
to the fruition,
from the sparkle
to the bright grey,
from the prayer book
to the missile,
from the song
to the order,
from the chanted rune
to the red telephone,
from the Latin
to the American,
from the delicate seas around Iona
to the girls leaning on rails
gum-chewing
towards America,
from the silence
to the murmuration of menace,
from a holy man in a holy cell
to a poised man in a poised cell,
from one light to another,

from the hive of the Ten Commandments
to their conversion into the binary system.

from TRANSPARENCIES

(3)

The old lady's head nods endlessly, without speech.
Not to be able to control yourself
is another loss of freedom, is another
way for the bars to cross.
She has no teeth.
Some slant of the white face
recalls the hull of youth.

(7)

Does the Renaissance
mean red pictures?
Or a brute snake
casting its skin?
Or a child in
perfect amazement blowing
purple bubbles
and trying
to clutch them?

(10)

Across the water,
blue land.
Nothing rooted.
From this distance
not inhabited.
Just land.
The light can colour
it any colour
it minds.

(11)

Roses in every garden—
an excess.
We are not worth this—
It isn't worth us.

If we had earned roses,
they wouldn't seem so strange,
so fat, so huge.
They'd have taken their place
like thistles,
an instinctive knowledge.

(21)
In the evening
the sea seems to come home:
after its great adventures
it speaks quietly
with a spare force.

(31)
I would love
to write
a 'great' poem,
big as the Cuillins.
Instead,
I sniff a yellow rose,
a great yellow
bourgeois
garden
rose.

And I stick a
carnation in my
buttonhole.
Deep red inside,
pink outside.
I thrust my cuffs out.
They are like the blur
of autumn
at the edge of a
leaf.

(32)
They come off the buses
ready for their dates,
handbags, smoked glasses.

O Via Appia,
via dolorosa,
via Romagna.

The light drains off,
the shadows
sleep in patient rows.

O via dolorosa,
La Scala,
our ladder.

Tons and tons of roses.

O the empty bowl
of Helensburgh.

(33)
The clock ticks
in the centre of a calm cloud.
Binoculars
in thin hands.
The fleet's gone now
over the horizon.
Elsewhere, it begins again
an empire,

involved and green,

swarming,

a shiny,

luxuriant,

paperweight.

(34)

Ah, how the yachts
thread in and out
such elegance,
such cardboard Marathons.

Blue,
red,
and the white ghosts
that slide in between

and the green
weed
pushes up
between the stones
nosing the incredible oxygen
which breeds such variations

from the elephant's bone
to the sea's
swaying,
delicate,
Hamletish,
fern.

from BY THE SEA

(1)

Sitting here by the foreshore day after day
on the Bed and Breakfast routine

I cower in green shelters, watch the sea
bubble in brown sea-pools, watch the sea

climb to the horizon and fall back
rich with its silver coins, its glittering.

Warmly scarfed, I almost remember how
beggars were, and in the thirties men

jumped from the wheel. I lock my will
on the National Health Service, will not fall

too deep for rescue but for the mind, the mind.
Two clouds loom together and are joined

as are two lovers in their nylon wings,
a yellow flutter on cramped bench. Thick rings

of routine save us, rings like marriage rings.
The yachts seem free in their majestic goings

and the great ships at rest. Helmeted girls
emerge from salons with their golden curls.

(3)

These hundred-year-olds preserved in glazed
skin like late apples. Where the yacht's guns blaze
they're startled in their shelters. Past MacNair—
Celtic's pre First War full back—they can share
tales of long-shirted footballers, rotate
on a fabulous bitten park. O the huge weight
of time's dead failures. (What would you say my age . . .
What would you say my age was?) Pipers wage
a mimic war. Eight and two drummers seem
a hired-out autumn at the minimum
cost to the town. These centenarians know
each blade of grass, each veer of yacht, each slow
seepage of the tide. God's ancient spies
and vultures of the spirit they surprise
by the teeth's grip on meat, persistent fangs
which have outanchored wives, their busy goings.

(6)
DUMBARTON

They're pulling down the Bingo hall today.
Crash! Through the glass the pole breaks to the walls
of the converted picture house. The stalls
and ornate balcony (once so outré
with its cheap cherubs of the Music Halls,
Victorian children, plump and neatly gay)
crack in white plaster on white overalls.

Where it once stood, a new smooth road will curve
to a late-night bar, pink with its lights and gin.
There will be leather seats, corners for love,
and the newly-learned cuisine
for the European progeny of those grave
unshaven unemployables who spun

one butt-end out, a river-side conclave

spitting in dirty water: who could get
their Marxist heaven from the plush back-row
watching the jerky stars in scratchy light,
who then would in soft twilight rise and go
half-swimming to the park and there would sit
eating their oily chips, the to-and-fro
of hard tall collars cutting at their throats.

(8)
AFTER THE GALE

The stunned world stops on its axis.
Slowly the clouds venture out.
The hills steady.

O Rome, duty was not enough—
the fixed spear, the savage mask for farmers,
the sentry in his place.

The upright eaten by the circular
spin of the stormy world, Hades uprooted
by a bright removal van,

the gods turned to pictures on the carnival
rotating with its fixed masks, its wolves
still upright in their chairs.

111

(10)

DUNOON AND THE HOLY LOCH

The huge sea widens from us, mile on mile.
Kenneth MacKellar sings from the domed pier.
A tinker piper plays a ragged tune
on ragged pipes. He tramps under a moon
which rises like the dollar. Think how here

missiles like sugar rocks are all incised
with Alabaman Homer. These defend
the clattering tills, the taxis, thin pale girls
who wear at evening their Woolworth pearls
and from dewed railings gaze at the world's end.

from THE WHITE AIR OF MARCH

(1)

This is the land God gave to Andy Stewart—
        we have our inheritance.
There shall be no ardour, there shall be indifference.
There shall not be excellence, there shall be the average.
We shall be the intrepid hunters of golf balls.

Have you not known, have you not heard, has it not been reported
that Mrs Macdonald has given an hour-long lecture on Islay
and at the conclusion was presented with a bouquet of flowers
by Marjory, aged five?
                        Have you not noted
the photograph of the whist drive, skeleton hands,
rings on skeleton fingers?
                        Have you not seen
the glossy weddings in the glossy pages,
champagne and a 'shared joke.'
                        Do you not see
the Music Hall's still alive here in the North? and on the stage
the yellow gorse is growing.
                        'Tragedy,' said Walpole, 'for those who feel.
For those who think, it's comic.'
                        Pity then those who feel
and, as for the Scottish Soldier, off to the wars!
The Cuillins stand and will forever stand.
Their streams scream in the moonlight.

112

(2)

The Cuillins tower
clear and white.
In the crevices the Gaelic bluebells flower.

(Eastward
Culloden
where the sun shone
on the feeding raven.
Let it be forgotten!)

The Cuillins tower
scale on scale.
The music of the imagination must be restored,
upward.

(The little Highland dancer
in white shirt green kilt
regards her toe
arms akimbo.
Avoids the swords.)

To avoid the sword
is death.
        To walk the ward
of Dettol, loss of will,
where old men watch the wall,
eyes in a black wheel,
and the nurse in a starched dress
changes the air.

The Cuillins tower
tall and white.
March breeds white sails.

The eagle soars.
On the highest peaks
The sharpest axe.

(8)

The exiles have departed,
                    leaving old houses.
The Wind wanders like an old man who has lost his mind.
'What do you want?' asks the wind. 'Why are you crying?
Are those your tears or the rain?'
I do not know. I touch my cheek. It is wet.
I think it must be the rain.

It is bitter
to be an exile in one's own land.
It is bitter
to walk among strangers
when the strangers are in one's own land.
It is bitter
to dip a pen in continuous water
to write poems of exile
in a verse without honour or style.

(9)

There have been so many
exiles.
          Jews
turn on their limited space
like cows.
          So many
faces blank as watches
telling
          nothing but time.

How can you drink a cup of wine
without tasting the vinegar
without feeling the thorn?

On the high far
Cuillins
I see them climb.

114

(12)

The tall buses pass by.
    The cottages trail their roses.

Look at the witch at the waterfall.
    She does Bed and Breakfast.

'Ah, Freedom is a noble thing.'

    Around the Cuillins
the clouds drift like green dollars.

(15)

The Cuillins tower high in the air—
                  Excellence.
We climb from pain to perfume:
the body opens out; gullies,
crevices, reveal the orchis.
The soul flies skyward,
impregnated with scent.
On the right hand
    the sun will tenant
Skye.
      The mist dissipates.
Gold grows at our feet.

(16)

    Excellence!
'costing not less than everything'
Illusion after illusion dies.
After the gay green, the blackness.
Snatches
'and I mysel in crammasie.'
Rainbows
out of the darkness.
Green,
green moments
or out of the waterfall
a sudden face—
so dearly known and killed.
Minotaur of guilt

coiled at the centre, vivid.
Flashes.
Blades.
Rotors of Glasgow knives.
Irises
held over tenements
intent, inventing,
Periphrases,
white deer stepping by Loch Lomond side.
The dead bury their dead.
The machines finished
underground.

In the white air of March
 a new mind.

(Between Comedy and Glasgow)

Translated by the author

MEMORY

Though we will not return home again
to that island,
we will always see the sun on the lochs,
we will not comb our hair without remembering
the wind on a dark moor.

THE QUESTION

You standing by a tree, a crown in your hand
of the flowers of spring, cold with dew.
'Why did Orpheus leave Eurydice?'
The dark days, the days that would come,
tall grey days without one picture.

CONVERSATION

'You wish to leave me, I can tell.
Though you do not know it, you wish to leave me.
I can tell it from your face and from your manner.'
I did not say anything. I was like the tree
losing its foliage, wanting to be bare again,
without, I believe, the music of birds.

IN THE MUSEUM

Together in the Museum—
I saw you with a stone in your hand.
You were on distant shores, you were alone,
though the brine was bringing tears to my eyes.

THE VISITORS AND GAELIC

The visitors are always talking about boats
their red shirts like their sails.
I am looking out through a window and seeing
black barbaric boats with black sails
with GAELIC written on them, leaves of autumn
—a sale, I am thinking, on a proud brown sea.

THE PROVERBS

The proverbs sailed
to a quiet harbour
where the other boats
were. Where they all were,
a village of brown sails,
drying in the sun.

IF YOU COME AGAIN

If you come again remember to bring with you
a mirror in which you leave your reflection,
a clock that will not move,
an armour without heat that I can wear.

IN THE CALM DAYS

In the calm days
they would quarrel.
They are alone
in the calm days.

WE WILL MEET

'We will meet sometime,'
he said,
'in a place without anxiety,
in an innocent village
where there will be calm without end.'

118

She didn't say anything.
She felt the ice
from that strange place
and the spiritual stars
making her breast cold.

SIX HAIKU

(1)

There is snow on the mountains.
I know a Japanese professor
who speaks Gaelic.

(2)

A piano in the desert,
Beethoven at a ceilidh—
Salvador Dali.

(3)

A wheel turning,
a melodious darkness,
a Gaelic record.

(4)

An angel at a door.
Sarah and Gabriel:
'Will you take tea?'

(5)

An old woman washing
the steps of a cinema—
above her, Greta Garbo.

(6)

A girl with nylons
walking past a prison—
the poetry of William Ross.

119

ON A MISTY EVENING

On a misty evening
I raised my luggage
on my shoulder
and I went on board the
Kaiora.

The guns began
to thunder
about Europe
on that large sea
where I was striving,
for Garrabost.

How red the water.
How red the brine.
No-one told me
about those roses
about those roses
that are swimming

about your son's cap, mother.
Your head of bone
is looking out to Salamis.
You are weeping ceaselessly.
The Kaiora is going down
at Trafalgar, at Bataan.

I WILL TELL YOU
WHAT HAPPENED

I will tell you what happened.
I was on a pavement in Glasgow
when I saw
shining on a wall
'The ripening moon of the barley—
she will take us home to Lewis.'

120

That was strange wasn't it
at Christmastime—
no Highlander was to be seen,
there was nothing but a skin
of white and red and green
and around me the empty street.
Anyway it brought to my mind
peat stacks, sea and fire
etcetera

And one night as well
as I was lying in my bed
I saw the Kaiora sailing,
as if it was on a morning
of summer, across the dresser—
and the room as white as crowdie or milk—
you understand—with the moon.

But greatest miracle of all
(I work in an office)
instead of the papers
with which I deal
I saw one morning
'The White Swan' written
firmly on my desk.

Well, I am sane enough,
that, anyway, is my opinion.
But it's strange
to live in a town
and to be walking through streets
so yellow and empty
and seeing coloured songs
but, well, I'll have to tell you
yesterday itself I saw
written clearly on a wall
BUY BRITISH BUY HAIG
and above it
    THE OAKEN STICK.

GAELIC STORIES

(1)

A fisherman in wellingtons
and his sweetheart
and his mother.

(2)

A story
about an old man
and a seal.

(3)

A woman
reading a Bible for seven years
waiting for a sailor.

(4)

A melodeon.
A peat stack.
An owl.

(5)

A croft.
Two brothers.
A plate with potatoes.

(6)

A girl from Glasgow
wearing a mini
in church.

(7)

The sea
and a drifter,
the Golden Rose.

(8)

A man who was in Australia
coming home
on a wedding night.

(9)
A romance
between cheese
and milk.

(10)
Glasgow
in a world of nylons
and of neon.

(11)
Two women
talking
in a black house.

(12)
A monster
rising from the sea,
'Will you take tea?'

(13)
A comedy
in a kitchen
with jerseys.

(14)
A conversation
between a loaf and
cheese.

(15)
A conversation
between a wellington
and a herring.

(16)
A conversation
between fresh butter
and a cup.

(17)
A conversation
between Yarmouth
and Garrabost.

(18)
A moon
hard and high
above a marsh.

WHEN YOU LEAVE ME

When you leave me
the dresser will return to its usual place,
the table will go nearer to the wall,
the images of the mirror will go out.

When you come back
I see a large ring of flowers,
a perfume rises from the wood,
the fire blossoms with roses.

THE DAYS ARE PASSING

The days are passing,
we are growing old.
What happened to the dancer in the mirror
with the cloudless face?
The twittering of the birds is further away,
drowned by the humming of the razor,
the towel behind the door
is like a ghost.

Ah, world, did you trick us
or was it that we did not rightly understand you
in those young days
when your face was open
reflecting our own faces?

124

THOSE LONG DAYS

Those long days,
those long Sundays,
years back
sitting on chairs
watching the fire going out,
the windows without story,
watching the grass growing,
without TV or radio,
and the soldiers dying
in countries without a mirror.

THE TV

(1)
The sun rises every day
from moving shadows—
on the TV.

(2)
We did not believe in the existence of Ireland
till we saw it many nights—
on the TV.

(3)
He knows more about Humphrey Bogart
than he knows about Big Norman—
since he got the TV.

(4)
Said Plato—
'We are tied in a cave'—
that is, the TV.

(5)
A girl came into the room
without perfume without expression—
on the TV.

(6)
At last he lost the world
as Berkeley said—
there was nothing but the TV.

(7)
He bought 'War and Peace,'
I mean Tolstoy,
after seeing it on the TV.

(8)
When he switched off the TV
the world went out—
he himself went out.

(9)
His hands did not come back to him
or his eyes
till he put on the TV.

(10)
A rose in a bowl on the TV set,
the things that are in the world,
the things that are not.

(11)
He found himself in the story.
He was in the room.
He didn't know where he was.

(12)
You, my love, are dearer to me
than Softly Softly
than Sportsnight with Coleman.

(13)
'In locked rooms with iron gates'—
but, my love,
do they have TV?

VI

RETURN TO LEWIS

(1)

The hills are stony as they've always been
with narrow roads and wide blue lochs between
and the bowed women carrying peats in creels
and tourists spread on grass at picnic meals
and buzzards hunched on fence posts bent on prey
and boys on bicycles and girls at play.
No houses now are thatched. Museums show
the curtained beds, and byres of long ago,
the tall old lamps, the griddles, and peat fires,
the wooden cart wheels before rubber tyres,
oars for the hands of giants, and low chairs
made from rough planks washed up on earlier shores.
Cows munch among the buttercups, and sheep
lie at the roadside almost sunk in sleep.
Tinkers subdued to council houses learn
to live as others do, earn as they earn
and English growing as the Gaelic dies
describes these vast and towering island skies.
God is surrendering to other gods
as the stony moor to multiplying roads.
Folk songs and country westerns in the bars
displace the native music sweet and harsh
which dilettantes soon will learn to prize
when the last real brutal singer dies,
too zealous and too tearful. Ah, those eves
of fine September moons and autumn sheaves
when no-one knocked on doors, and fish was free,
before the Bible faded to TV
and tractors ground the bones of horses down
into bone-meal well suited to the town,
and girls were simple who drink brandies now
and wear mascara who would milk the cow.
But times have changed, and steamers bring to shore
cargoes of cars, that brought just men before,
and drivers in black glasses burn the miles

129

between waning townships and diminished schools
where children learn what education's for—
to look from elsewhere to a well-loved shore
and leaving home wave to the tourists who
set off each summer into hopeful blue.

(2)

This old black pot is boiling with the soul.
The sea is quivering for mile on mile
with jellyfish and eels. The island seethes
with all the dead. It will not let us breathe
with the old crying 'Alas' and all the drowned
who were given water but no inch of ground.
I hear that sea, God's voice, all afternoon
as my hurt eyes are prickled by the sun,
thorns of descending rays. The men in black,
the women in wheeled hats, go past the rock
to where the children bathe. The sea resounds
all day about me, and it grinds and grinds
dead seagulls down to grit, dead crows to sand.
Sheeps' bones are lying handy to my hand,
and canisters and bottles. This vast voice,
luminous with fish, will never cease
till everything is fined to where it sprung,
churches and hats, the bell's colossal tongue,
and boats that crack along the world's long shore,
beneath the sky's indifferent decor.

(3)

Time hangs heavy here. On certain days
you could cut it with a knife or dip a spoon
into its heavy porridge. 'Where is Ann?
What happened to that fellow-what's-his name?'
The boat butts through it, and that hooded dame
fights hard against it, till it beats her down.
Houses rise against it to a town,
lean late to villages. And the summer bees
hum it insistently where the clover grows,
red heather and bog-cotton. Cows and sheep
collapse within it, and the cemeteries keep
it close and warm. The waves return it to

130

shores which are grey and then are sparkling blue.
Stones throb with it, and straw, and roofs which fall
among the thistles and sustaining wall.
Sundays that ache with it endure for years.
Roads aimlessly follow it to broken piers.
Young girls like vases swell with it, then crack
some winter's morning, and it bows the back
of aged men and women: and it ticks
in clocks and watches, as in candle-wicks,
though sometimes, dearest, on fine autumn nights
it pauses momently and across the straits
the moon casts chains of an unending gold,
the breasts like waves seem never to grow old,
the poignant sheen of an eternal world.

(4)

This is the place I grew in. Barefoot, I
would run to school under a summer sky
on the grass beside the road. Today I see
far larger houses each with its TV
aerial on the roof and at most doors
or in their garages new glittering cars.
The moor smells heavy as it used to do
and skylarks rise from nests. My town-made shoe
squelches among the moss. I've travelled far
from this small village by its sandy shore
with its ruins of thatched houses, roofless walls.
The girls I knew are wearing women's shawls.
The fields seem smaller, and the Standing Stones
diminished now against less wide horizons
which once were bounds to simpler, slower minds.
The grass is waving now in stranger winds
and I feel sorrow more than I feel joy
as all must do who see the phantom boy
that they once were, scrambling among the pools,
in his breeze-filled jersey, or among sea shells
entirely concentrate. No-one can return
ever again to the place where he was born
who once has left it. Perhaps better so.
My feet accelerate to swift from slow
as if pursued by ghosts that in the breeze
seethe like the fish in these rich northern seas.

131

(5)

All night the wind blows round the house, and rain
in from the Atlantic beats the window pane.
The voices keen around me in my bed
where I shake at shadows as if the long dead
in black and green were haunting me. I feel
someone beside me under this sheet and squeal
like a rabbit in a trap. I feel my eyes
under the seagull's beak, as it swiftly flies
down through the skylight rattled by the wind.
Beneath these stony eyes I am made blind
threshing in water, and its ruinous green.
I am bewildered by this bleak machine
whose wings, salt with the ocean, flap my head
laid bare and briny on this shifting bed,
pale herring of eternity, fixed at last
by this cold sword which pierces through the blast.

(6)

Down on the sand the visitors turn brown.
Their children plunge in roaring waves that bring
the blue shells shoreward, and whose uttering
is not in Gaelic but an idiot tongue
relentless and obscure no poet's sung
nor slant-capped peasant decent by his fence
rooted in time and grass and reticence,
while the sky curves from moor to treeless moor
and the only colour is his painted door.
The squealing children rush the waves and run
pursued by water towards the white sun
which broils their parents to a crablike hue.
I gaze intently into that large blue
astounding acreage imagining the seals,
blunt-headed sharks, and the gigantic whales,
in playful motion while here deep in grass
the cows munch endlessly and packed mini-cars
wait for the tourists whose sand-castles fade
into the ocean's blind monotonous trade.

'I'll tell you something, lad' he sits and says.
'What do we mean by it, "the good old days"?
Left school at twelve, I did. Six in our class.
Many's the time my ears were boxed. I was
a great one for horses. All I'd want was plough,
plough, plough, forever. There are no horses now
hardly in the island. As for cows—
you'll never see one round a village house—
we import our milk. I'll tell you something else,
I took a fancy to the bicycles.
I'd leave it in the town when I'd had some beer,
it was always there when I'd go back, no fear.
Then in the war I was on the Murmansk run—
as cold as death. A corvette, thirty men.
A two and a half ringer commanded her—
you'd have to cut the ice from off the wire—
we were nearly buggered many a time. But yet
I tell you this, you never can forget
the "good old days," when you were young, you see.
No responsibilities. Many a day
I'd burst out laughing and my mates would stare.
I'd be laughing at what happened in the year
1912 or so, you understand. . .
The rest thought I was daft or just half-canned.
My mother's 93, you see. She's got
all her facilities. We told her that
seven more years she'd get a telegram from
the Queen herself. And all she said was "Hm
What good is that to me?" I had to laugh.
Honest, when you think of things, you'd have
to see the funny side. I played the pipes.
And yet there's Calum, one of the best types,
a great accordeonist, and they found him dead
the other-day lying in his bed.
Cancer and thrombosis. Nothing but that.
And Peggy Ann, she's grown so stout and fat
who had a figure like an hour glass once.
And Seumas Black who walked just like a prince
hobbles about, but yet in rain and shine
you'll see him visit Iain. '69
I retired from work. I wake at four o'clock
just on the dot and light a fag or smoke
my pipe, and lie and think. I've never yet

133

burnt the bedclothes. That's a fact. I met
the minister yesterday and he said a thing
I've thought of since (it gave me a good sting)
"Men need a compass, not a weather cock."
And that's true too. It would put you on the rock.
Well, anyway good night. You see that moon?
You'd hang your hat on it. That's a good sign.
"The good old days." I tell you, they were that.
When you are thin you think you'll not get fat.'

SHALL GAELIC DIE?

(Translated by the author)

(1)

A picture has no grammar. It has neither evil nor good. It has only colour, say orange or mauve.

Can Picasso change a minister? Did he make a sermon to a bull?
Did heaven rise from his brush? Who saw a church that is orange?
In a world like a picture, a world without language, would your mind go astray, lost among objects?

(2)

Advertisements in neon, lighting and going out, 'Shall it . . . shall it . . . Shall Gaelic . . . shall it . . . shall Gaelic . . . die?'

(3)

Words rise out of the country. They are around us. In every month in the year we are surrounded by words.

Spring has its own dictionary, its leaves are turning in the sharp wind of March, which opens the shops.

Autumn has its own dictionary, the brown words lying on the bottom of the loch, asleep for a season.

Winter has its own dictionary, the words are a blizzard building a tower of Babel. Its grammar is like snow.

Between the words the wild-cat looks sharply across a No-Man's-Land, artillery of the Imagination.

(4)

They built a house with stones. They put windows in the house, and doors. They filled the room with furniture and the beards of thistles.
They looked out of the house on a Highland world, the flowers, the glens, distant Glasgow on fire.

They built a barometer of history.

Inch after inch, they suffered the stings of suffering.

Strangers entered the house, and they left.

But now, who is looking out with an altered gaze? What does he see? What has he got in his hand? A string of words.

(5)

He who loses his language loses his world. The Highlander who loses his language loses his world.

The space ship that goes astray among planets loses the world.

In an orange world how would you know orange? In a world without evil how would you know good?

Wittgenstein is in the middle of his world. He is like a spider. The flies come to him. 'Cuan' and 'coill' rising.*

When Wittgenstein dies, his world dies.

The thistle bends to the earth. The earth is tired of it.

(6)

I came with a 'sobhrach' in my mouth. He came with a 'primrose.' A 'primrose by the river's brim.' Between the two languages, the word 'sobhrach' turned to 'primrose.'

Behind the two words, a Roman said 'prima rosa.'

The 'sobhrach' or the 'primrose' was in our hands. Its reasons belonged to us.

(7)

'That thing about which you cannot speak, be silent about it.' Was there a pianist before a piano? Did Plato have a melodeon? Melodeon in the heavens? Feet dancing in the heavens? Red lips and black hair? Was there a melodeon in the heavens? A skeleton of notes.

(8)

'Shall Gaelic die?' A hundred years from now who will say these words? Who will say, 'Co their?'† Who? The voice of the owl.

(9)

If I say 'an orange church' will I build an orange church?

If I say 'a mauve minister' will I create him?

The tartan is in its own country.

The tartan is a language.

A Campbell is different from a Macdonald (this is what a tartan teaches).

The tartans fight each other. Is that why they had to put a colourless church between them?

(10)

Said Alexander Macdonald, 'It was Gaelic that Adam and Eve spoke in that garden.' Did God speak Gaelic as well, when he told them about the apple? And when they left that garden, were they like exiles sailing to . . . Canada?

*'Cuan' means 'sea' and 'coill' means 'wood.'
† 'Co their?'—'Who will say?'

(11)

Shall Gaelic die! What that means is: shall we die?

(12)

An orange church with green walls. A picture on a wall showing ships like triangles. On another wall, a picture of a cafe with men made of paint. 'Gloria Deo' in the language of paintings, an orange bell, a yellow halo around the pulpit where there are red dancers.

(13)

Were you ever in a maze? Its language fits your language. Its roads fit the roads of your head. If you cannot get out of the language you cannot get out of the maze. Its roads reflect your language. O for a higher language, like a hawk in the sky, that can see the roads, that can see their end, like God who built the roads, our General Wade. The roads of the Highlands fit the roads of our language.

(14)

When the ape descended from the trees he changed his language. He put away the green leaves. He made small sharp words, words made of stones.

(15)

The dove returned to Noah with a word in his mouth.

(16)

The scholar is sitting with a candle in front of him. He is construing words. He is building a dictionary. Little by little, inch by inch, he is building a dictionary. Outside the window the children are shouting, a ball is rising to the sky, a girl and a boy are walking without language to bed. What will he do when the ball enters the quiet room, breaking the window, stopping him at B, and Z so distant.

(17)

Whom have you got in the net? Who is rising with green eyes, with a helmet, who is in the net?
Cuchulain is in the net, he is rising from the sea, ropes of moonlight at his heels, ropes of language.

137

(18)

'When you turn your back on the door, does the door exist?' said
Berkeley, the Irishman who was alive in the soul.
When the Highlands loses its language, will there be a Highlands,
said I, with my two coats, losing, perhaps, the two.

(19)

A million colours are better than one colour, if they are different.
A million men are better than one man if they are different.
Keep out of the factory, O man, you are not a robot. It wasn't a
factory that made your language—it made you.

(20)

Like a rainbow, like crayons, spectrum of beautiful languages. The
one-language descended like a church—like a blanket, like mist.

(21)

God is outside language, standing on a perch. He crows now and
again. Who hears him? If there is a God let him emanate from the
language, a perfume emanating from the dew of the morning, from
the various-coloured flowers.

(22)

Death is outside the language. The end of language is beyond
language. Wittgenstein didn't speak after his death. What language
would he speak? In what language would you say, 'Fhuair a'
Ghaidhlig bas?'*

(23)

When the name 'Adam' was called, he turned his back on the hills.
He saw his shadow at his feet—he drew his breath.

(24)

You cannot say, 'Not-Adam.' You cannot say 'Not-Eve.' The apple
has a name as well. It is in the story.

(25)

The gold is new. It will not rust. 'Immutable universal,' as the
Frenchman said. But the pennies, the pounds, the half-crowns, these
coins that are old and dirty, the notes that are wrinkled like old faces,
they are coping with time; to these I give my allegiance, to these I
owe honour, the sweetness. 'Immutable, perfect,' Midas with his
coat of gold and of death.

*'Fhuair a' Ghaidhlig bas'—'Gaelic is dead.'

FOR JOHN MACLEAN, HEADMASTER, AND CLASSICAL AND GAELIC SCHOLAR

(1)

The coloured roses fade along the wall.
How shall we live? How perfectly they fall,
the October leaves in yellow, how exact
the woods appear, so married to the fact
of their own unwilled and accurate funeral
without interrogation. In this tract

the dazzling hearse has led us to, we stand,
hats in our hands. The serious piper plays
'The Lament for the Children' and we hear the bound
and ribboned bouquets thudding. Then we take our ways
to the waiting cars across unechoing ground

or over crackling gravel. It remains,
the body in the casket, and begins
its simple mineral weathering. We return
to our complex human burning. What we mourn
changes as we mourn it, and routines
wed and enring us as we move and burn.

(2)

For you it was the case that Homer lived
in our fluorescence, that Ulysses homed
through our stained and plaguey light, that Hector grieved
in his puncturable armour, that engraved
even in Skye was marble which consumed
the bodies of live Greeks who shaped and carved

contemporary sculpture. Under leaves
which dappled your warm garden (as the groves
of autumnal classic Greece) you turned a page
or made an emendation in a passage.
Exactitude's a virtue, so believes
the inveterate scholar. Happy who can judge

evil as a hiatus or a false
quantity in harmony, who knows
that what protects us from the animals
is language healthy as a healthy pulse
and that our moral being can like prose
be manifestly tested where it fails.

(3)

I know that it is waning, that clear light
that shone on all our books and made them white
with unanswerable grammar. That the slaves
sustained our libraries and that the wolves
and watchful eagles nourished an elite
and that the elegant and forceful proofs

of their geometers will not suffice.
I know that Athene is wandering now,
dishevelled in the shrubbery, and the nurse
beckons at evening to her. Gods rehearse
their ruined postures and the ruined brow
reflects from mirrors not of fire but ice

and that our brute Achilles drives his wheels
across the gesturing shadows: and that kneels
to cheering legions Aphrodite: packs
are watching Ajax hacking with his axe
inanely the pale sheep: and shady deals
illuminate Odysseus's tracks.

(4)

You were a teacher also: what we've learned
is also what we teach: and what we are
cannot be hidden, though we walk black-gowned
along the radiant corridors, profound
in serious scholarship and that precious star
proposed by art or conscience. Where you burned

exactitude prevailed, the rule of Rome,
the gravitas of Brutus and his calm,
his stoic tenderness, his love of books,
his principles and practice. For the Dux
stands in his place, the overwhelming psalm
enchants him wholly among clean-limbed Greeks,

and if you touch him he gives out true coin.
Echo on echo, pupils make a world
which is their bronze and yours, and they will join
link on bright link to make the legions shine
with ethics and with elegance. The absurd
becomes a simple weather, clear and fine.

(5)

The October leaves are falling. None condemns
their seasonal abdication. What consumes
their crowns and robes is natural, a law
that's common to the weasel and the crow.
They hear no music of the funeral drums
and no corteges shade the way they go

no mountains brood, nor does the sharp wind mourn
nor tragic clouds move slowly. For the ice
steadily thickens over lake and corn.
In this pure azure there's no paradise
nor the hell nor purgatory that we devise
lest in the world we shiver and we burn

without the falcon's unhistorical aim,
its brutal beak, the momentary tomb
of its spontaneous moments. Or the sheep
that grazes in its own forgetful sleep
or the barbarians that struck at Rome,
its pompous destiny and shadowed hope.

(6)

Though it is finished now, that scholarship,
though vases crack and hourly we may graze
on superficial quanta: though we sleep
abandoned to disorder, and the days
are flashes of small light: and what we praise
is transient and odd, we yet may keep

pictures of autumn, graver, more restrained,
with a finer balance of the weighty mind,
a wind from Rome and Greece which held our course
steady to a harbour where salt oars
received their justice and to scales assigned
the soul would shiver with a stronger force

141

which now in neon vibrates. But in light
(let it be legend) accompanied the leaves
to their natural assignations and the fruit
bowed to a holy earth. The swan that moves
in reedy waters bows its neck. The waves
receive it, flesh and shadow, day and night.

(7)

So with your battered helmet let you be
immersed in golden autumn as each tree
accepts its destiny and will put by
its outworn crown, its varying finery,
and let the humming of the latest bee
bear its last honey home. Beneath this sky

the hexagonal coffin crowned with flowers restores
your body to the earth from which we came
to build our shaking ladders. What was yours
was no phantasmal order, and your name
planted in this place held to its aim
from wider deeper origins. If there were pyres

then a pyre you should have had, and lictors too.
And phantom legions. In this perfect blue
imagine therefore flame that's amber, yellow,
leaves of good flame, volumes that burn and glow,
the foliage of your autumn, where you grew
and where you are buried in the earth you know.

VII

ON A SUMMER'S DAY

Thus it is.
There is much loneliness
and the cigarette coupons will not save us.

I have studied your face across the draughtsboard.
It is freckled and young.
Death and summer have such fine breasts.

Tanned, they return from the sea.
The colour of sand, their blouses the colour of waves,
they walk in the large screen of my window.

Bacon, whose Pope screams in the regalia
of chairs and glass, dwarf of all the ages,
an hour-glass of ancient Latin,

you have fixed us where we are, cacti able to talk,
twitched by unintelligible tornadoes,
snakes of collapsing sand.

They trail home from the seaside in their loose blouses.
The idiot bounces his ball as they pass.
He tests his senile smile.

THE MOON

The bronze curtains hang at the window.
Between them the moon is shining like a bell.
It is an eye that has been there forever,
a Greek eye older than Pericles.
It looked upon Oedipus and taught him how
the intellect should investigate the flesh,
the rustlings in the shrubbery. It burned
the armour from Greek boxers, those pale statues
that inhabit dense groves. It is the eye
of Sir Apollo, the clear operator,
doctor and sun-god, of the theatre
the radiant master, scooping out the eyes.

OEDIPUS AND OTHERS

The god Apollo scratched out both his eyes.
Tragedy is light too bright to bear.
There were no choices in that azure heaven,
no mercy, only justice. Daughters, sons,
projected death unto the third generation.
Death was everywhere, it was a plague.
The reasonable man became obsessive,
the formal beard was stained with blood, and Creon
forced the young student to the barricades.
From king to rebel, the crystal wheel rotates.
Thin in the light, in vibrant quivering black
Antigone throws the book at Creon, dies
in an ecstasy of longing. Creon says:
'The king must rule, that's what a king is for.'
Oedipus sleeps in the groves of wise Athens.
The light burns fiercely on a public stage.
They're all proud germs the theatre must kill.

GOOD AND EVIL

'Good' is not like 'yellow' or like 'green.'
There are no traffic lights that one can stop at.
The soul has many roads and all different.
Frankenstein nails the bride to the wall
and vampires swoop like Zeros. But 'good' is not
—nor evil either—clearly what we see.
'Good' sits like a nun but is not a nun
it's not the collar of the perishable.
Electricity is waiting in the house.
I enter it from the snowstorm. I switch on
the bulb that glows above my battlefield.
The furniture springs quite clear as we spring clear
from the dreadful dark of strata, murderous pools.
God switched it on and suddenly we shook
in bald vibrations in that merciless light.

OVER AND OVER

They came from him at night in the light of Homer.
Their pistols glittered on the hexameters.

They shot him when the verse was in his mind
of Hector dying, and the chariot wheels

went click click click. In the black leather
he saw Troy burning, and a clear small face

with large round spectacles, barrelled in the light
of the study's genial fireplace. He got up

to pick the book, leathered in black, and then
there was the knock and they came in again.

DEAD FOR A RAT

What snarls
in the corner?
It wants to live
It bares its teeth at you.

It wants to live
more than you do
Its whole body
trembles
with its want to live.

The fur arches from its body
Its green eyes spark
Its lips are drawn back from the teeth
It hates you.

It hates you
more than you hate it.
Hamlet
lie down
in the sound of the trumpet

It quests you Hamlet
Will you go
behind the arras
behind the tapestry
will you go
Hamlet
with all the weight
of your bright thought
upon you?

Will you go Hamlet
in your shuttling armour
in your whirr
of literature
with your French rapier
sparkling, veering?

from CAROL AND *HAMLET*

Small and small-breasted you scribble in your jotter.
Shakespeare must be known. One needs a Higher
to get a job suited to father's daughter—
or even unsuited. There is a fire
pours through the long windows, causing water
to dance on the wall. From my tall chair
I wonder who perhaps Ophelia was
in her own world apart from Shakespeare's gaze

and the whole lot of them in their private places
before a public tragedy made them pure
and dragged Ophelia from her own oasis
into our own world and into literature
and what you are—beyond hypocrisies—
and I on this unsteady hovering chair.

*   *   *

That leaf you see touching the window now—
I mean in summer—where has it come from?
How old's the tree from which it swam and swam
upward to here? O deep and deep below
this grey stone building can you hear the worm
turning and writhing, hissing, a red fire,
an orchestra of worms about the bare
and brittle skull which still has kept its form?

We ride above them in our little ship.
How many gowns have rustled past that door
containing now an actor, now a bore,
now a great Roman, now a huddled shape,
and yet that leaf is fresher than we are,
green with the green of a transparent grape.

*   *   *

149

That's why Hamlet always talks of death.
Beyond the ruffs and doublets he saw it clear.
Outgrowing the Renaissance's bright air
he saw instead of wigs the curling wreath.
Below the foam he saw the depths beneath
as you perhaps, a rural visitor,
camping with Girl Guides may see pools where
eels move and flash and coldly whip and writhe

below the dappling sunlight where we live.
I saw it once, an eel, dead-white, upright,
like a blind dancer drifting in the light.
It was so different I couldn't grieve
for such a death so distant and so white
I shivered in the whiteness of my grave.

*   *   *

I too was terrified of words once.
I was so frightened of where words would lead me
that I would walk at night over the stones
(yellow with moonlight) and feel fear beside me
as palpable as a yellow snarling dog
or a yellow rat. The night was wholly yellow.
Inside me a perpetual monologue.
Outside me the whole yellow town was hollow

including the Square, the Post Office (now shut)
the yellow kiosk and each yellow footfall.
I feared each clicking motion of my foot
and felt below me a huge echoing well
where language sent each yellow writhing root
which, had I known it, would grow green and cool.

*   *   *

DEAR HAMLET

Dear Hamlet, you were pushed beyond your strength
you had a white face and black clothes,
you stood at corners listening.

Surrounded by the voices and wondering what you should do.
The old father whom you admired so much
but who had driven you to Wittenberg
lay murdered.

To avenge him when you did not even like him
(though you admired him) wasn't easy.
He had won so many battles but you,
you had won none.

Poor schoolboy, longing to be like your father,
learning to fence when he had used an axe,
learning philosophy because he hadn't done so.
Words are not enough.

Rushing about from one commandment to another
you were finally focussed as a target
by Claudius, the small and simple man,
yes, he was simple.

So little sufficed him, just a queen, a kingdom,
salutes from guards, dinners with dinner-jackets,
bow-ties and crowns, the glitter of cut-glass,
the colour of poison.

But you, you needed more. That more was death.
You chewed it, fed on it, watched for it in mirrors,
hunted the castle for it, loved it the best
of anything you had known.

How silly Fortinbras was, not to see it
standing behind him just as he took the crown.
That was the moment he began to die
and you began to live.

HOW OFTEN I FEEL LIKE YOU

Ah, you Russians, how often I feel like you
full of ennui, hearing the cry of wolves
on frontiers of green glass.
In the evening
one dreams of white birches and of bears.
There are picnics in bright glades and someone talking
endlessly of verse as if mowing grass,
endlessly of philosophy round and round
like a red fair with figures of red soldiers
spinning forever at their 'Present Arms.'
How long it takes for a letter to arrive.
Postmen slog heavily over the steppes
and drop their dynamite through the letter-box.
For something is happening everywhere but here.
Here there are Hamlets and old generals.
Everyone sighs and says 'Ekh' and in the stream
a girl is swimming naked among gnats.
This space is far too much for us like time.
Even the clocks have asthma. There is honey,
herring and jam and an old samovar.
Help us, let something happen, even death.
God has forgotten us. We are like fishers
with leather leggings dreaming in a stream.

from RUSSIAN POEM

(1)

I am too old for you.
Nevertheless
in summer under a crown of leaves . . .
I am in debt,
a kind of Hamlet.
Nevertheless,
Sonia, you are beautiful.
I've left my Jewish wife
mooning from piano to vodka.
She coughs all night.
You do not know the guilt . . .
Here in the sunshine it is fine,
you in your white dress. . . .
People, such people.
Generals
with false red faces
booming like snipes.
Old uncles, aunts,
surplus to requirements.
Sonia,
there was a time
when I had ideals.
Now my back is broken.
I feel nothing, Sonia,
even should you put
lightly your hand in mine,
even should you kiss
I'd not awaken.
Sonia, I'm afraid
of this old skin.

(3)

Hear us. Philosophy will not save us.
In our salons we have talked the 'soul' to death.

Our cigar smoke snakes from the orchard
where the apples ripen and the small hands

shine.

Our glasses reflect the sunset. Our monocles
have a raw glare. The uncles

twinkle like robins.

We have talked the 'soul' to death. Now as the sun goes down
we shiver and go in.

(4)

Gogol, how your troika sparkled down our leaf-fringed lanes.
You stopped at the most absurd houses
where everyone was himself and dullness sparkled like genius.

Moral bachelor, what has happened to you? You have run to history
for protection. You have abandoned your people.
You have run your little troika into the wilderness.

(5)

In the siding the red light veins his beard.
The rails run elsewhere, hard and narrowing.
Our land breathed through you. Now you are breathless.
Your soul is blown sideways by the steam.

I look down the track at the raw torches
wandering hither and thither. What do I see?
Is it the mad city face of Dostoevsky?

154

(10)
Sonia, my fine ghost,
I see you among the rifles.
You were saying 'What need of a psychiatrist?
He would only stare at my wrist.'

Sonia, you were a sign of the times,
a young girl vibrating out of phase.
I see you wearing white slacks,
legs spread apart,
reading old leaves.

Sonia, you were a generator
bouncing on a piece of waste ground.

Sonia, it has come at last.
The newspapers have gone mad.
They are punching out Reality.

If I do not die now I shall die.

Sonia, I stretch out my hand to you.
I am afraid but I stretch out my hand to you.
Sonia, let us follow the wind.

PARTY

Cigarette ends mounting slowly in the ashtray,
so many Hamlets speaking all at once.
'Polonius is a fool to have such power.'
I leaf through Bacon's paintings in the corner,
a butcher's shop of graduated screams.

Now they are dancing on the charred carpet.
You can tell the lost ones from their stiff arms.

The others sway to the music just like snakes.
'He's nice to me but never says he loves me.
He strokes his car's flanks over and over.'
She waggles her bum, a green suburban mermaid,
flicking her fingers, Venus of the record player
half hidden by the fog, the swirling grey.

DIPPING YOUR SPOON

Dipping your spoon in the mash of TV
palls. Everything palls. Spy and detective stories,

watching your cold small face on its seventh gin,
hearing the ringing jokes from bell-like faces,

writing great novels on white tablecloths.
What is given is not enough to make us swing
happily on branches or to climb
these long stone stairs, watches bobbing on chains.
We want the Commandments from the gritty deserts

and shadowy ghosts in their post-Renaissance frames,
our underwater programmes. We want your Commandments
suited to a pastoral land in green,
the extinct shepherds with their pilgrim staffs,
their clouds of white sheep and visiting angels
perching on branches with their fathomless eyes.

SHANE

He comes out of some place where he has invented justice.
What is good has to be protected by guns
and that is why he's so sombre. Why his silence
grows on the bustling housewife who asks about fashions.
He has learned a style from evil, he has honed it on
conflict. He knows that books will not save
the innocent man. He stands by the fence
undazzled yet alert, expecting evil
as natural as sunlight. Yet with what grief he goes
to find his guns again, to relearn his quickness.

END OF SCHOOLDAYS

Captains, this is your last day in school.
You won't wear these helmets any more.
Do you not hear the whisper in the triumph,
like a suspect heart? Do you not see
how Mr Scott, though kind, is harried
by voices inaudibly calling from his house.

Look out on the fields. Never again will you see
such a sweet greenness, as of colours leaving
a place where they've been happy for a while.
The harness is turning now to other horses.
Laughter comes up the road and mounts the brae.
The names on the doors are rewriting themselves.

Never mind, the music will not leave you
or not completely. Sometimes in a betrayal,
in the middle of a deal just turning rancid,
after the fifth gin, the fifth fat hand,
the cloudy globes, set on the cloth, you'll hear it,

the music of your Ideal, quietly humming
in locker-rooms that smell of sweat and rain.
You'll be coming home in a warm and eerie light,
legs tall and willowy, in your hand the cup,
shaking a little, in your flabby hand
the trembling cup, in your old grasping hand.

FOR KEATS

Genius is so strange,
you were in so many ways ordinary
in so many ways wounded like us.

But the vase beckons—
continually the vase beckons—
the imperfect bird sings
in the brown mortal leaves.

Poor Tom dies in the white linen.
Sore throats! Do nightingales have sore throats?
In the nightingale's pure notes
What eloquent disease?

Happily to seek the classic—
that land without fatigue—
that which stands like the rocks of Staffa
black remarkable architecture of the sea
solider than weeping Skye.

Than the grass of summer,
devotees of England's spas,
the irritabilities of the second rate,
the helmet bruised and vain.

Fighting the scree, to arrive at Autumn,
innocent impersonal accepted
where the trees do not weep like gods
but are at last themselves.

Bristly autumn, posthumous and still,
the crowning fine frost on the hill
the perfect picture blue and open-eyed
with the lakes as fixed as your brother's eyes,
autumn that will return

and will return and will return, however
the different delicate vase revolves
in the brown mortal foliage, in the woods
of egos white as flowers.

GAELIC SONGS

I listen to these songs
from a city studio.
They belong to a different country,
to a barer sky,
to a district of heather and stone.
They belong to the sailors
who kept their course
through nostalgia and moonlight.
They belong to the maidens
who carried the milk in pails
home in the twilight.
They belong to the barking of dogs,
to the midnight of stars,
to the sea's terrible force,
exile past the equator.
They belong to the sparse grass,
to the wrinkled faces,
to the houses sunk in the valleys,
to the mirrors
brought home from the fishing.

Now they are made of crystal
taking just a moment
between two programmes
elbowing them fiercely
between two darknesses.

IN THE CHINESE RESTAURANT

Because we'd never go there, it was good,
those years together. We'd never need to go
though we could talk of it and so we were
happy together in a place we'd made
so small and airless that we couldn't leave.
But we could think of it and say, 'Perhaps
we'll go there someday.' But we could not go
for as we lived so we'd lost all the maps.
It grew more perfect as the slow years passed
as if we were there already. One fine day
we'd find it all around us if we looked.
We would be in it, even old and grey.

So that, one night, in that late restaurant
with Chinese waiters round us we picked up
the menu in Chinese and understood
every single word of it. It was
a revelation when the waiters smiled.
They looked so clear as the glasses slowly filled.

THE SMALL SNAGS

The small snags tug at us. The flag will not unfold
glorious in the weather of our triumph.
It is the small snags that won't let go.
For if the flag unfolds and leaves the earth
and is pure spirit, a wide heavenly cloth,
then earth will not remember us but fade
with its arrangement of small serious weasels,
its rats with clear green eyes, its stoats and foxes,
the thickets that entangle as we move.

Let not the flag unfold too widely, let not
the hero in his brilliance, let not
the silk unwind its soul's advertisements,
but be like clothes snarled in the summer hedges
where the birds sing clearly from their dying mouths
and the owl snaps through its folds.

160

CHILDREN IN WINTER

In the dark mornings
the orange-coloured children
test the black streets
hand in hand.

The darkness pours down.
The moon is leaning backwards
like an exhausted woman.

They fade into their future,
like small orange sails
breasting the darkness.

CHRISTMAS 1971

There's no snow this Christmas . . . there was snow
when we received the small horses and small cart,
brothers together all those years ago.
There were small watches made of liquorice
surrealist as time hung over chairs.
I think perhaps that when we left the door
of the white cottage with its fraudulent icing
we were quite fixed as to our different ways.
Someone is waving with black liquorice hands
at the squashed windows as the soundless bells
and the soundless whips lash our dwarf horses forward.
We diverge at the road-end in the whirling snow
never to meet but singing, pulling gloves
over and over our disappearing hands.

IN THE TIME OF THE USELESS PITY

In the time of the useless pity I turned away
from your luminous clock-face in the hopeless dark,
appealing to me greenly, appealing whitely.
Nothing I could do, I had tried everything,
lain flat on the rug, fluttered my spaniel paws,
offered you my house like an unlocked crystal—
and so it came, the time of the useless pity
when the roots had had enough of you, when they slept,
elaborating themselves by themselves
when they shifted over from yours, seeking a place
different from yours to burst through and to pierce
with a royal purple, straight and delicate: sails
of the suave petals unfurling at the mast.

FINIS NOT TRAGEDY

All is just. The mouth you feed turns on you
if not truly fed, the machine clicks
accurately in a new house.

The will that you abolished stands slackly
when you need it most, the vanquished
muscles will not answer.

The machine, powered by history, clicks
shut like a filing cabinet and on it
you read Finis not Tragedy.

Nothing is there that wasn't there.
No memos that you haven't read
over and over again

when your skull-faced secretary stood smiling
as you tore papers into little pieces
and hummed through your clenched teeth

and turning you said to him 'Remember honour.
Tell the story as it really was.'
But he is silent, smiling.

162

EVERYTHING IS SILENT

Everything is silent now
before the storm.
The transparent walls tremble.
You can hear the very slightest hum
of a stream miles away.

The silence educates your ear.
The threat is palpable.
You can hear the boots beyond the mountains.
You can hear the breathings of feathers.
You can hear the well of your heart.

You know what it is that permits the walls,
that allows the ceiling,
that lets the skin cling to your body,
that mounts the spiral
of your beholden bones.

That sorrow is a great sorrow
and leaves you radiant
when the tempest has passed
and your vases are still standing
and your bones are stalks in the water.

THIS GOODBYE

This goodbye
was the closing of two doors,
the dimming of two circles.

This goodbye
was not an assembling of
precious souvenirs.

This goodbye
happened so quickly I
was not aware of it.

It was just that I was not looked at.
It was just
an injustice of the glass.

VIII

from ELEGIES

YOU LIVED IN GLASGOW

You lived in Glasgow many years ago.
I do not find your breath in the air.
It was, I think, in the long-skirted thirties
when idle men stood at every corner
chewing their fag-ends of a failed culture.
Now I sit here in George Square
when the War Memorial's yellow sword glows bright
and the white stone lions mouth at bus and car.
A maxi-skirted girl strolls slowly by.
I turn and look. It might be you. But no.
Around me there's a 1970 sky.

Everywhere there are statues. Stone remains.
The mottled flesh is transient. On those trams,
invisible now but to the mind, you bore
your groceries home to the 1930 slums.
'There was such warmth,' you said. The gaslight hums
and large caped shadows tremble on the stair.
Now everything is brighter. Pale ghosts walk
among the spindly chairs, the birchen trees.
In lights of fiercer voltage you are less
visible than when in winter you
walked, a black figure, through the gaslight blue.

The past's an experience that we cannot share.
Flat-capped Glaswegians and the Music Hall.
Apples and oranges on an open stall.
A day in the country. And the sparkling Clyde
splashing its local sewage at the wall.
This April day shakes memories in a shade
opening and shutting like a parasol.
There is no site for the unshifting dead.
You're buried elsewhere though your flickering soul
is a constant tenant of my tenement.

167

You were happier here than anywhere, you said.
Such fine good neighbours helping when your child
almost died of croup. Those pleasant Wildes
removed with the fallen rubble have now gone
in the building programme which renews each stone.
I stand in a cleaner city, better fed,
in my diced coat, brown hat, my paler hands
leafing a copy of the latest book.
Dear ghosts, I love you, haunting sunlit winds,
dear happy dented ghosts, dear prodigal folk.

I left you, Glasgow, at the age of two
and so you are my birthplace just the same.
Divided city ot the green and blue
I look for her in you, my constant aim
to find a ghost within a close who speaks
in Highland Gaelic.
                        The bulldozer breaks
raw bricks to powder. Boyish workmen hang
like sailors in tall rigging. Buildings sail
into the future. The old songs you sang
fade in their pop songs, scale on dizzying scale.

IN YOUR LONG SKIRTS

In your long skirts among the other girls
you stand beside the barrels, leather-gloved,
in 1908 or so, with severe lips.

The girls are all dead and you are dead.
Two wars have happened since and many fish
have bred and died in the cold North Sea.

In that brown picture you all look very old
for twenty-year-old girls and you're all gazing
to a sun that's off the edge and is made of salt.

YOU TOLD ME ONCE

You told me once how your younger brother died.
It was by drowning. In the tar-black sea
he sang a psalm to bring his rescuers near.
That did not save him though. One cannot hide,
you would have said, from destiny. So here
there are two meanings working side by side.

You died of lack of oxygen. I tried
to fit the mask against your restless face
in the bumpy ambulance in which you lay.
I thought that moment of the psalm as guide
beyond our vain technology, the grey
and scarlet blankets that you tossed aside.

MY SAILOR FATHER

My sailor father died in hospital
of a consumption, forcing you to burn
all your furniture and begin again.
Chair and table blossomed in a hail

of memories which set him in the cordage
of a white schooner setting out to sea,
its sheets unfolding, moving carefully,
the trousseau and red roses of your marriage.

169

THAT ISLAND FORMED YOU

That island formed you, its black-hatted men
and stony bibles. How your father's beard
streamed like a cataract. And the heart's devoured
by the black rays of a descending sun.
Always they're making fences, making barred
gates to keep the wind out, their slow pace
deliberate and punctual. Who has heard
of the terrible cyclones that infect deep space?
The daffodils are yellow on the wind
but in these souls where is the love, my dear,
to dally in fine leisure as the clear
smoke rises from the houses, and the cock
shrills redly from the waste abundant air?

ALL OUR ANCESTORS

All our ancestors have gone abroad.
Their boots have other suns on them. They died
in Canada and Africa with God,

their mouths tasting of exile and of spray.
But you remained. Your grave is in Argyll
among the daffodils beside a tree

feathery and green. A stream runs by,
varying and oral, and your will
becomes a part of it, as the azure sky

trembles within it, not Canadian but
the brilliant sparklings of pure Highland light.

YOUR BROTHER CLANKED HIS SWORD

Your brother clanked his sword for the Boer War.
Also in Egypt, later still in France.
We won't have much of that continuance.

There'll be no more of that old clattering
among red poppies in a crowded room
of antique ornaments won at Imperial fairs.

Our skies are clearer and more deadly now,
our hell is all around us in the blue
bubble over Hiroshima, our rooms

more pared to their essentials, the chairs
swaying in a purer breeze, the sun
climbing forever to a shriller place.

THOSE WHO ARE NEEDED

Those who are needed do not easily die
or those who think they are needed. When your face
turned to the darkness it was as if the sky
took to itself its light. There were in space
no lightnings from a god. No apples fell.
No new significance present to our slides
keeled from a distant planet and no bell
swung anywhere one could hear. Or if it hides—
some heaven somewhere—with its level blue
and lack of gradient, it's beyond this ship
that through our atmosphere serenely glides
bearing intelligence and anguish too,
its natural pains, the honour that we keep
with ourselves or heaven or our compass guides.

ON LOOKING AT THE DEAD

This is a coming to reality.
This is the stubborn place. No metaphors swarm

around that fact, around that strangest thing,
that being that was and now no longer is.

This is a coming to a rock in space
worse than a rock (or less), diminished thing

worse and more empty than an empty vase.

The devious mind elaborates its rays.
This is the stubborn thing. It will not move.

It will not travel from our stony gaze.

But it must stay and that's the worst of it
till changed by processes. Otherwise it stays.

To beat against it and no waves of grace
ever to ascend or sovereign price

to be held above it! This is no hero. This
is an ordinary death. If there is grace

theology is distant. Sanctify
(or so they say) whatever really is

and this is real, nothing more real than this.
It beats you down to it, will not permit

the play of imagery, the peacock dance,
the bridal energy or mushrooming crown

or any blossom. It only is itself.
It isn't you. It only is itself.

It is the stubbornness of a real thing

mentionable as such and only such,
the eyes returning nothing. Compromise

is not a meaning of this universe.
And that is good. To face it where it is,

to stand against it in no middle way
but in the very centre where things are

and having it as centre, for you take
directions from it not as from a book

but from this star, black and fixed and here,
a brutal thing where no chimeras are

nor purple colours nor a gleam of silk
nor any embroideries eastern or the rest

but unavoidable beyond your choice
and therefore central and of major price.

OF THE UNCOMPLICATED
DAIRY GIRL

Of the uncomplicated dairy girl
in gown that's striped in blue and red
feeding the hens in a windy spring
by the green wooden shed
where shade after quick shade
endlessly shuttles let me speak
and speak unsorrowing.

As in the weather of a Lewis loom
a pastoral picture, striped against the blue,
against the stone, against the green,
against the cottage with its daisies
taking the place of roses
casting the meal from a young hand
still without its ring.

The long dress billows in the breeze
mixed like the confectionery
you'd bring home from the fishing
in the large yellow chest with hats,
silken things and coats,
just before your straight-backed brother
marched off to save the King.

Just stay there therefore for a moment,
uncomplicated dairy girl,
in your chequered screen of red and blue
holding the pail in your hand
before the sky is red and mooned
and feathered by (beyond the dance)
the beat of metal wings.

THE BURIAL

The coffin is let down into the grave,
the honey-coloured hexagon's not glass.
I hold a tassel. Past my locked cold face
the little rain goes slanting. It is love

that moves the black sun and the black stars.
It's love that makes my body tremble like
a shorn and meagre ewe when it is struck
by the winds of heaven and it shrinks and cowers.

These verses spoken through the driving rain
do not prevent the coffin's slow descent.
The ribboned wreaths thud on the wood. I stand
confronted by a single vivid scene,

your face in the open coffin, fixed and stern,
rebuker of mortality, incised
to a cold hauteur that I half recognized
as seen on coins or Presbyterian iron.

TINILY A STAR GOES DOWN

Tinily a star goes down
behind a black cloud.

Odd that your wristwatch still should lie
on the shiny dressing table

its tick so faint I cannot hear
the universe at its centre.

THE LILIES AND THE DAFFODILS

The lilies and the daffodils shade your face.
They show and do not hide your old bones.
This is your land, this is where you will die,

where the wind blows over and over your hair,
where your dreams sink by inches every year,
where the lilies and daffodils will rise from your bones.

175

CONTRASTS

Against your black I set the dainty deer
stepping in mosses and in water where
there are miles of moorland under miles of air.

Against your psalms I set the various seas
slopping against the mussels fixed in place,
slums on the ancient rock in salty rows.

Against your bible I set the plateau
from which I see the people down below
in their random kingdoms moving to and fro.

Against your will I set the changing tones
of water swarming over lucid stones
and salmon bubbling in repeated suns.

Against your death I let the tide come in
with its weight of water and its lack of sin,
the opulent millions of a rising moon.

THE CHAIR IN WHICH YOU'VE SAT

The chair in which you've sat's not just a chair
nor the table at which you've eaten just a table
nor the window that you've looked from just a window.
All these have now a patina of your
body and mind, a kind of ghostly glow
which haloes them a little, though invisible.

There is, said Plato, an ideal place
with immortal windows, tables and pure chairs,
archetypes of these, as yet unstained.
In such a world one might look out to space
and see pure roses yet untouched by hand,
the perfect patterns of a universe

of which our furniture is but editions
bred from a printing press which has no end.
The perfect Bible will remain unread
and what we have's a series of translations
which scholars make, each nodding aching head
bowed over texts they never can transcend,

and yet more lovely because truly human,
as tables, chairs and windows in our world
are ours and loved because they taste of us.
Being who we are we must adore the common
copies of perfection, for the grace
of perfect things and angels is too cold.

So in this room I take the luminous
as being the halo of our sweat and love
which makes a chair more than a simple chair,
a table more than a table, dress than dress,
and startlingly striking out of the air
the tigerish access of a crumpled glove.

THE EARTH EATS EVERYTHING

The earth eats everything there is.
It is a year and a half now since you died.
Your marble tombstone stands up like a book.
The storms have not read it nor the leaves.
The blue lightnings bounced from it.
The ignorant swallows perched on its top.
I have forgotten it over and over.
Life is explainable only by life.
I have read that on paper leaves.

177

NO ONE AT HOME

There is never anyone at home when I call.
Through the wrought railings I can see your study
through the pale window but you're never at home.
I leave your house and walk the street again.
They are hooking men at the open air draughtsboard
and I hear soft music playing in the Gardens.
The mind has terrifying labyrinths.
'Wherever you wander, O wherever you roam
there is no place as terrible as home.'
Restless you prowl the streets, your learning lodged
with the snakes of your brain's attics. I remember
you standing with a cocktail in your hand.
You were as white as an eel I saw once,
upright in the water, almost dead.
It was an angel of the endless waste.
You are an angel whose bubbles are all gone.
Your thousands of books waterfall the walls.
You pressed a name and a bell would once ring.
Now there are no bells: you've pulled the wires.
The citizens walk their dogs in the evening,
their bell-shaped faces ruminant and red.
They do not know enough to be so tired.

I THOUGHT I SAW YOU

I thought I saw you on the street just now
in your biscuit-coloured slacks. It wasn't you.
Nothing will ever die, not even lies.
The taxi's meter clicked. There was a view
of Glasgow's ruinous land of green and blue.
When will the heart learn better enterprise?

Hotels receive me. What receives your ghost?
What elevator, station, road or slum?
The mind has tricks that we are desperate for.
How can we turn away? There is no home
other than it, and where you go or come
is here or elsewhere but is always here.

THE WORLD'S A MINEFIELD

The world's a minefield when I think of you.
I must walk carefully in case I touch
some irretrievable and secret switch
that blows the old world back into the new.

How careless I once was about this ground
with the negligence of ignorance. Now I take
the smallest delicate steps and now I look
about me and about me without end.

THE BOUQUET

You brought me a bouquet, salt with brine.
Neither was it your fault. The sea is salt.

The sea is darker than anyone dares to know.
The lights more bright for vaster distances.

179

ON THE TRAIN

Nothing is cool and green any more.
My brain could burn that ashtray where it stands
on the table that this train is carrying north.
Outside there is a greenness and big stones,
hills that go on forever, brawling streams.
But the rails are heating, they converge on something.
Logic has failed us. We are burning up.
The adored days are bowed on other lakes.

WHERE ARE YOU TONIGHT?

Where are you tonight as the rain falls?
Are you reading interminably in your room
as a child does in the shadow and the flame?
Remember that game that we played together
on another day of wet dark weather
naming in the bookshops all the books we'd read.
I hadn't read Du Maurier nor you Ballard.
We are not the kind who can ski or ride.
Sometime long ago we were sent to bed
and held the page up like a tombstone
which later was our fascination and our pride.
To communicate in quotations . . . Some do that,
as if they were facsimiles of other men's thoughts,
footnotes explainable by scholarship.
We are like asterisks in the shady sky
and more translatable than poetry.
I see you bowed in the rain over
your green and humming leaves forever
child, reader, insatiable sister,
phantom of a book, holding a book in your hands.

AT THE SCOTT EXHIBITION,
EDINBURGH FESTIVAL

(I)

He will outlast us, churning out his books,
advocate and historian, his prose
earning him Abbotsford with its borrowed gates,
its cheap mementos from the land he made.
Walking the room together in this merciless
galaxy of manuscripts and notes
I am exhausted by such energy.
I hold your hand for guidance. Over your brow
the green light falls from tall and narrow windows.
His style is ignorant of this tenderness,
the vulnerable angle of your body
below the Raeburn with its steady gaze.

(II)

It was all in his life, not in his books
'Oh I am dying, take me home to Scotland
where I can breathe though that breath were my last.'
He limped through an Edinburgh being made anew.
He worked his way through debts, past a dead wife.
My dear, we love each other in our weakness
as he with white grave face diminishing through
stroke after stroke down to the unpaid room.
We know what we are but know not what we will be.
I tremble in this factory of books.
What love he must have lost to write so much.

from POEMS FOR DONALDA

HELPLESSLY

Helplessly I wait for you.
I think I am nothing without you.
I am like a grey street on which the sun rises
and suddenly there is a noise of cars
the cries of flower sellers
the shaking out of antique pictured rugs.

LOVE, DO NOT LEAVE ME

Love, do not leave me.
I could not bear it.
I could bear it
but it would be hard.

There is little that cannot be borne
even dishonour,
even the power
of not bearing parting.

Which is worse to bear,
love responsible
or the empty glamour
of being reasonable,

the daily struggle
to keep love entire
or with hauteur
call it trivial

to preserve the noble
heart from breaking
to covet the aching-
admiring one's will?

THE PRESENT

I brought you a green belt
out of green Ireland
and a Galway shawl
which is black and holed

and when you put them on
you seemed both old and young
as Ireland itself is
in its right and wrong

with its proud body
and its ancient head,
a fierce witty lady
subdued by the dead.

'THE THINGS I DO'

'The things I do,' you said, 'injecting sheep,
cutting up, stacking logs with a power-saw,
chasing a neat white goat out of a field.'
You do them with such gaiety. After all,
to you they're possible, for you have done them.
But as for me, to write another poem
is not so easy as to cut the grass
now that the grass grows nearer and less green.
I wish, I wish . . . And once there was a cottage
white with its daisies like an old man's beard
and violets I trembled to walk over.
Departure seemed inevitable, so
the mind's a power-saw endlessly munching wood,
and chasing a white goat across a field.

THE SHADOWS

'I think,' she said, 'we shall not see again
each other as we did. The light is fading
that was once sunny in the April rain.
Across the picture there appears a shading
we didn't notice, but was in the grain.'

The picture shows two people happily smiling
with their arms around each other, by the sea.
Whatever they are looking at is beguiling
themselves to themselves. There is a tree
with orange blossoms and an elegant styling

but they are lost quite clearly in each other.
They do not see the landscape, do not hear
the stream that tinkles through the azure weather.
It's as if really the clear atmosphere
were a creation of two souls together.

But at the back there steadily grow two shadows
one for each lover that they can't evade.
They emerge threateningly from the coloured meadows
as if they were a track the two had made
and they were ignorant of, their changeless natures.

And as they move the shades intently follow
growing steadily darker, spreading as they go
as the wings' shades pursue the flying swallow.
My dearest love, if these should make us slow
remember late the first undying halo.

IX

THE ISLAND

'And as for that island,' so he said,
'we shall remember it always however we change,
the sun on the lochs on a clear day.
We shall not comb our hair without remembering
the windy grass on the moor.'

SKYE

Stone and rain and mist on the mountains.
The calm straits extend everywhere without sails.
The minister in black drowses in his manse.
Once they say there were thirteen hundred souls
on Raasay. Now there are one hundred.
The Isle of the Roe Deer is corruptly beautiful.
Whose is the blind dog with the green eyes
sniffing among the thorns? The silence is cruel.
It makes the old faces thin and pale.
Here time munches comfortably. Look out to sea.
A live sheep, deep in the brine, stands with drenched wool.

from ISLAND POEMS

(1)

KILNAVE CHURCHYARD, ISLAY

In this calm place the graves are very old,
the writing almost illegible. Many men
are lying here with their wives and children,
families reconciled in stone
under the earth's green billows. As we read
in the loud sound of the Atlantic
a lark flies straight up singing. There's a grave
newly open with a spade inside it.
A large hare leaps from behind a stone
and dashes crazily from us. The sky holds
us and the dead, our flesh and the old stones,
some of which are bare of writing.
Imagine how in winter the wind howls
round the unwritten stone, unglamorous, poor.
But now the world is totally calm.
The Atlantic glitters gaily. My hand is warm
leaning on this stone. My shirt is rippling.
The hare has gone to ground, the lark is singing.
The dead knew this joy, they are part of this joy now.

(3)

AN ISLANDER SPEAKS

I was born in this village seventy years ago.
I have ploughed my land, I have harvested.
I know everyone to the bone, they know me.
We are, to each other, open doorways.

I was married to a village girl.
I have ploughed my land, I have harvested.
Her motions were of the sea, now of the land.
Her grave flesh entrances me more each day.

You say, 'I am sad leaving the island.'
The ship rises and falls
away from, towards the gulls.
We sink into a sleep which heals
us of the island's distance
from the mainland's rushed nerves.
When later we waken
it'll be different again
we shall be ready to enter
by that harsher newer door.

THE VOICE

I hear in this valley which is loud with streams
a voice that cries, 'You are a guilty sinner,'
and this is what the desolate Highlands mean.
'Guilty, guilty,' that voice cries and cries
though the delicate deer don't hear it, they don't raise
their heads out of the grass, and the sheep feed
steadily, contentedly. But the voice
grows louder and louder endlessly passing sentence
from the black mountain peaks that tower around
and saying in the noise of flowing waters,
'Guilty sinner, when will you ever see
the blackness of the stone, in the rhododendrons
the devilish snake uprising, in the sunset
the blood of the long-judged who burn with Me?'

THE PROCESSION

Clad all in black, they bear the coffin over
a moor of heather, early daffodils,
in the noise of running streams and early birds.
They are stiff and squat, emblems of sombre Sundays,
with their hard black hats that bite into their brows.
They are a frieze against a pulsing landscape,
against a sky of free and moving cloud.
They lay the coffin down and rest themselves
and as they do so the glass lid springs open.
A daffodil arises, clear and tall,
with its faint bells of yellow, soundlessly ringing,
casting its colour on their sombre clothes.

IN THE DARK

Feeling across a field in the dark
one shields one's eyes against the wire fences.
The body tenses and the eye winces,
the feet feeling for ditches draw back.

And we remember that all our art
is dependent first on light and then on skill,
for how could any poet go to school
in a black field with such a checked stride?

Inching sometimes over unsteady stone
and by a black stream waiting, hearing its noise
and guessing from its small or major voice
how deep it is, how shallow, how serene,

aching intently for magnanimous light
which is the page and the reason for the page
the space which tempts us out to voyage
beyond the field, beyond its fenced limit.

THE GLASS OF WATER

My hand is blazing on the cold tumbler.
My eye looks through it to the other side.
If it were what is real, if it were heaven
how I corrupt it with my worn flesh.
How its neutrality is aggrandised
by fever and by empire. I constrain
and grasp this parish which is pastoral.

To be pure is not difficult, it's impossible.
How could the saint work to this poverty,
this unassumingness, this transparency?
How could his levels be so wholly calm?
The fact of water is unteachable.
It's less and more than honour standing up
invulnerable in its vulnerable glass.

POEM FOR AUDEN

When you died
it wasn't really like a dying,
you had done it so easily.

As your poetry is so easy
that one doesn't realise the many
zigzags you've contrived
to find your way through,

emerging like a magician with phrases
you seem to have picked up on hedges
on days luckily voracious
from the briary thorns of Old English
and the crooked spells of witches.

The sailor sets out in ice,
his harp sharp and shaggy.
He knows the hirpling monsters,
halls where the light falls,
and the doomed tippling lord
brooding on chessboard.

He learns Mozart,
the sea-knowledge of Freud,
has a face like an old map,
a dissolute pirate.

He tosses phrases like coins
while the moon blazes above him,
quizzical, humorous,
stunningly cold and bold,
absurd lovely Diana.

He turns away at the end
from all the tempests,
habituate to housework,
with a housemaid, an old dog,
and a radiant bathroom
where the body convicts the soul.

'The heel on the finishing blade of grass.'
Abruptly he enters the silence.
The sorcerer is laid in the wood
which will play forever.

ORPHEUS

(1)

And he said, I am come in search of her
bringing my single bitter gift. I have
nothing more precious to offer
than this salt venom seeming to you as love.
It is true I cannot live without her
since I am now shade who was once fire.
See, mineral spirit, how I now suffer
by the slow heavy motion of my lyre.

And the god then replying, Let her stay
for by her absence your music is more clear
barer and purer. Always in the air
her distance will perfect her as Idea.
Better the far sun of an April day
than fleshly thunder in the atmosphere.

(2)

And he said, That is great condemnation,
to live profoundly and yet much alone.
To see deeply by a barren passion.
It was forgetfully I moved the stone
which now submits to my examination.
She was my sense; around her flowing gown
my poems gathered in their proper season.
They were her harvest yet they were my own.

And the god then replying, What you say
is what her absence taught you. Our return
is not permissible to an earlier way.
If it were possible you would learn to mourn
even more deeply. Do you never burn
poems whose language was becoming gray?

(3)

And he to the god, If you should let her go
I'd know my music had its former power
to melt you too as once it melted snow
to alter you as once it altered her

192

so that in music we both learned to grow.
It was a dance of earth and of the air.
But up above it's easier. Here below—
The shade then smiled and said, Behold her there,

and he beheld her whitely where she stood
in that deep shade. She seemed not to have changed
nor he to have changed either as he played.
And yet her apparition was so strange.
She didn't fit the music that he made.
The notes and she were mutually disarranged.

(4)

And the god to him, Now I must tell you clear
what you refuse to see, since it is hard
to accuse ourselves of cruelty and fear.
You wished that she should die. And what you heard
was not my voice but yours condemning her.
If you will learn to love you must go forward.
For that is how it is in the upper air.
All that you have shared you have now shared.

And Orpheus took his lyre and left that place
and moved where the shadows moved and the clouds flowed
and all that lived had its own changing grace.
As on an April day there was sun and shade
but nothing vicious or virtuous
haunted the various music that he played.

(5)

And he to the god, Tell me about the shades.
Are they more real above or here below?
Or is it as with trees that stand by lakes
for looking downward you will see them grow
away from you in water. I would know
whether my lyre is real or whether it fades
as my hand fades or whether on my brow
a ghostly laurel as in water shakes.

And the god to him, They vibrate both together,
your lyre and such reality as there is,

193

each making each as in a misty weather.
The berries that grow richly on the trees
should be sufficient for you, whether these
are just themselves or shadows of each other.

And, for your lyre, though you might feel as shade
what I might feel as solid that is no
disturbance of the harmony you have made.
If I should rise to where you come and go
the stones and trees to me would be as shade
and the white water would in blackness flow
and my black lyre would shift and change and fade
as in the twilight hills of indigo.

And he to the god, But you have never climbed
to plead with me to have your love returned
from the shades of upper air in which she moves.
Now therefore I consider that I've burned
with a more real pain and that our loves
are dearer and more near for that attempt.

But the god was silent as in Orpheus's hand
the lyre expanded and contracted like
a shadow that's projected on a wall.
Slowly he extended through the black
atmosphere his arm and took the lyre
and played such music as the zodiac
if made of solid heavy massive chains might make
which yet were banked with elegies and fire

and Orpheus almost swooned against that force
as if the very blackness spoke in joy
with its own elegance, intense and sparse.
The motion was a boulder's yet the cry
so piercing and so pure that if he died
he knew his eyes would stream with sparkling tears.

(6)
And he to the god, I have descended from
the city of vibrations where I see
the beggar seated in alternate gloom
and negligent neon and continually

the concentrated faces in a dream
of their own separate force are passing by
as if in passion or delirium
since each of us is crying, 'I am I'

for life must generate its vanity
and from each window waves the personal soul
singing, If necessary let others die
but as for me I have the right and will
to my own measure of the present day,
however transient and however small.

And so I think I wish to stay with you
and lay aside my lyre and sleep at last
in a monotonous place where nothing new
troubles the spirit and with face aghast
I need not always stand against the tempest
making an adamant music, being true
to a lost captain and a mutinous crew
in an ugly and adulterated waste.

And the god to him, There is no way to stay
as if you were an engine which has drawn
its final string of carriages and in May
is found among the rails where marigolds burn
in rustic sidings miles and miles away
from the main headlong tracks of sparkling iron.

For I may tell you that it ends in rust
however in the summer it appears
pleasant and archaic and exposed
to the quaint gents who hunt for souvenirs
and potter in the sunshine of the past
for precious evidence of affectionate powers
which though tremendous weren't harshly used.

In any case your destiny hasn't ruled
that you remain below. You must return
as a good driver to the upper field
without a destination. You must learn
to read the flags more closely and compelled
by an ardour of the spirit always burn
forward on tracks continually rebuilt.

And Orpheus walked among the broken slums
whose windows had been smashed or cracked or boarded
and saw the children play among discarded
mattresses and boxes and the scum
of moist and dirty cardboard. There were poems
chalked on the flaking walls, misspelt, ill-worded,
and in the closes women with red arms
stood talking fiercely with their aprons girded

and his lyre was clouded as with greenish slime
and all the brilliant strings appeared corroded
by it and the monotony of time
and he might have ceased to play but that the sordid
stout valiant women so unkempt, sublime,
laughed gaily in the morning without hatred.

So that beyond the shade he saw the human
invincible spirit playing, as one goes
through utter darkness and sees water gleaming
and all the way one walks through resonant meadows
or as from a fast train by tenements racing
one has a glimpse of a white-vested man
plunging his vigorous head into a basin
beyond a sudden sparkling window pane

or children blowing bubbles by a shore
where dogs retrieve thrown sticks and someone writes
with unaccustomed pen, Wish you were here,
and girls stretched out on deck-chairs dream of nights
with Elvis Presley while their mothers share
with Valentino fading appetites.

And so his lyre had a graver heavier tone
as if containing all the possible grains
that can be found in marble or in stone.
What he had lost was the sweet and random strains
which leaped obliquely from the vast unknown
concordances and mirrors but the gains,
though seeming sparser, were more dearly won

as less in mobile warfare than in trench
one sees the faces closer as they loom

in their thorny helmets whether German, French,
or some quite other nation; and they seem
so like his own—the cheeks, the teeth, the chins—
that he must love them not as in a dream
but on this smoky field of green and orange.

LETTER

You say, 'I am alone. Are you alone?
All summer I have felt beneath the ground
my laurels hibernating. But what of you?
The nights are longer surely in the north,
more room to sleep, more room to keep awake.
Here in the town I famish for your stars.
My gown remembers what your dews are like.
I saw a book with pictures of an eel
swaying as if to music in a loch.
Have you a record of its briny soul?
Summer should see my soul quite whole again.
The dead should never write letters to the dead.
Green as a leaf I shall grow here for you,
the watermark of the paper that I send.'

IN THE GLEN

The stags come down from the hills and he comes over.
I do not want him for his wife says no.
There are a few houses and that's all,
and a mad gossip of an intellectual
who wears red clothes and a proud phantom crown.
I do not want him but I am alone.
He mends the car and breaks the wood for me.
But I do not want him for his wife says no
and we must live in this community,
dependent on each other. We are leaves.
I hear him coming as the stags come down
gently to drink at the pale evening water
steady and large, their antlers faintly shining.
I hear him crunch the gravel. Through the pane
I see his wife's eyes fixed at another pane.
I watch him coming. He has lost his shame.
I am his drug, he says. The intellectual
walks by the river in her splendid dream.
She thinks we're peasants and her mind is cold,
a heron by the river fishing for books
she read at Cambridge centuries ago.
The stags lift up their heads. The door lies open.
I sit here coldly by the trembling fire
from which I'd cast large rabbits on the wall
for my fatherless children sleeping overhead.
He's standing in the doorway. I am waiting.
I hear the drumming hooves. The heron's chased them.
His shadow climbs the wall and he is here.
He is so tall beyond my warm small chair.

CEILIDH

Some ragged tartans hang above the stage.
There are wooden trestles and they all come in,
the villagers, to listen to their past.
Some finished passion has removed all haste
and granted courtesy instead of rage.
The years have taught them how to lose not win.

Such sleepy faces gather for the dream.
Of this pure ceremony what might aliens think,
this late communion of the dispossessed?
Are they the best, or have the fiercer best
abandoned for real things the things that seem,
the suns that rise for the old suns that sink?

The music starts. Exile begins again.
They leave the mountains and the glens in song.
They are lost sailors on a moving mast.
The girls they sing of are all sweet and chaste,
herbs of the mountains, sighs of a dear Amen.
The stream of elegy receives all wrong.

The common dream unites them as they gaze
into the tender surfaces. They hear
the bagpipes playing from the wars they've lost
historically, daily. At what cost
would they awaken now and taste the day's
sharp bitter victories, barbarous and dear?

The overbred and overcivilised . . .
The accordeons and pipes are packed away
into their boxes and the songs are finished.
The decorated hall seems quite diminished.
Their souls return to what their souls have prized
too little against exile and decay

and they set out to real glens and hills
depleted townships and the gathering roar
of midnight streams, the moonlight on the sea.
They come together—Art and what they see—
but, should they leave, what new dream strikes and kills
knocking forever at a lustrous door?

THE SOUND OF MUSIC

After the *Sound of Music* we mooned out
into the street again. Glasgow by night.
The pavement and the road were blue and wet.
There wasn't a single rainy close without
a couple kissing. They wore narrow tights
and clung together in the plaguey lights
infecting their white faces. It was not
what one would call a fine attractive sight.
It was a whimpering wolfish appetite.

It wasn't really like the *Sound of Music*
with all those Viennese waltzes and the like,
the roomy castles, staircases, the stock
Hollywood airs and graces (not oblique)
of trilling nuns more musical than Catholic,
their sudden warbles, eloquent technique,
but everyone so cheery and so slick.
They seemed to sing whenever they should speak
and all so nice and pricey as in *Vogue*.

Through the blue and green of Glasgow we strolled on
by Indian restaurants and Chinese ones.
Cropped youths stalked past us in their mottled skin,
their glinting eyes expressionless as stone.
There was a dance-hall coloured violent green
and slogans six foot high made yellow stains
on rotting tenements. I could see no nuns
and nowhere marbled halls or chanting children
but swaying drunks so miserably alone

that convents could not reach them, nor God's ways
which chimed with Hollywood's refined arias
that even the gauleiters could not suppress.
The screen, uncracked by bottle or by vice,
reflected perfect flawless families.
I did not walk in fear but saw each dress
as in a radiance which I must prize
not freshly laundered nor as Viennese
but stained with sweat to a more tense repose.

200

INCIDENT

She watched him with her children and she thought,
'They're not his flesh. What am I hoping for?
They are my flesh and mortal, of myself,
they grew in me and by me, we are all
a chain of common growing, or a ring,
and of the days a wandering company
cohered in pain and happiness. But he walks
distant yet dear, not one of us. They run
together down the road. He sees them as
I see some other children, how they are
is not to me responsible, their grave
or playful motions not so far from me
as stones might be, but they are not my care
in sunshine or by lamplight, they are less
deeply embedded in me. So with him.'
She watched him walk, she knew his mind as clear
observer of the clouds and of the sky
and of the pale white moon that slowly rose
into the frosty winter afternoon.
The children ran ahead, competitive
in matching clothes, the fair one and the dark,
cowboys and transient tenants of that space,
their merciless energy inveterate
and normal in the day. She closed her eyes
and when she opened them she saw the three
bending over a pool of mottled ice.
She saw him break it tenderly with his shoe
pointed like a dagger while they stood
beside him watching. Then he turned and smiled.
His smile was white as the ascending moon
of equal delicacy and equal light.
Her smile strengthened to his, two partial moons
converging on the full and harvest moon
which lights the autumn corn. Then with rare joy
she heard them running towards her, and he
was walking steadily not away but to,
and she was the centre of the untidy chain
whose light was for the three, whose light was not
meagre and bristly but ubiquitous,
on them as always but on him as well,
and then on them, and him who from the clouds
had turned his eyes on her and the common earth.

AUTUMN SONG

'I'll be seeing you
in all the old familiar places,'
she heard a voice singing as she walked
among the autumn leaves.

Among the autumn leaves where there were no radios
only a voice that sang
more sweetly than the inhuman nightingale
of human days gone wrong.

THE OLD WOMAN

The old woman sat under an autumn tree.
She was not thinking of anything, she was thinking
of her tall sons who had gone away
in the large ship with white sails.
It grew steadily colder round the old woman
and her hands shook like the blown leaves
that weren't going anywhere particular
in the insistent motion of the autumn wind.
The white sails had sunk over the horizon
and her sons walked under other stars
pointed and poignant, high above their home.
But the old woman drew her shawl about her
in the cold air, in the autumn flutter
and became like the earth, part of the earth, became
a soft remembrance in a sharp land.

OLD WOMAN

'The Old Age Pensioners,' she said,
'are to be granted an extra pound.
It was stated by the Government.'
And this, I knew, had made her proud.
Now she'd more easily afford
residence in her own son's house.
And I, who had more than enough
to buy whatever she should choose—
her prudent spare necessities—
must in that luxury pretend
to be gladdened by such marvellous news.

For dignity is what we crave
when all else has been pared away
and we must sit each single day
or lie, as ready for the grave.
It is a way of being brave
and a diminished happiness
seems only diminished to the strong.
Tonight the tears came to my eyes
unbidden as I thought of this.
It was the ending of the day
and a white moon was in the skies.

SKETCH

The squashed church leans out of the thunderstorm.
His stubbly cheeks are gaunt, and the yellow corn

drums with a mental wind. When shall the flowers
be allowed to be themselves, when shall the vase

again contain them? The failed missionary
burns in his studio and will never marry,

for the paints reek of Van Gogh and when his mind
spins on itself the cornfield feels the wind.

THE PRODIGAL SON

'All day,' he said, 'I've been trying to write a play
about the Prodigal Son and how he came
home after twenty years on a fine day
to where his brother laboured in the corn
with his huge curving scythe that was the same
as he'd used the day the Prodigal Son had gone.

I tried each way. The Prodigal Son had prospered
while the farm slowly decayed as the huge scythe
steadily harped at the stalks where the wind whispered.
Or perhaps the Prodigal Son turned at the gate
and headed, humping his case, for the hated south
because his arrival was that much too late.

But somewhere in my mind there was a boulder
I couldn't climb or pass. A day so pure,
the weight of failure on each dusty shoulder,
the large forgiveness of that simple weather
seemed so beyond the power of literature
I couldn't focus on the happy father,

his outstretched arms grasping a changing ghost,
a harvest of images that the autumn brought
home to wherever home is for the lost.
It wasn't possible that the Son should come
or if he came that his grave wandering spirit
should settle there after delirium

as each new day perched on the rusty fence
and rotting posts and, radiant on ponds,
revealed more sparklingly unchanging essences.
Would he not leave once more when useless growth
barrenly blossomed, when the lying diamonds
momently flourished as ever from the scythe?'

CHINESE POEM

(1)

To Seumas Macdonald,
                    now resident in Edinburgh—
I am alone here, sacked from the Department
for alcoholic practices and disrespect.
A cold wind blows from Ben Cruachan.
There is nothing here but sheep and large boulders.
Do you remember the nights with *Reliquae Celticae*
and those odd translations by Calder?
Buzzards rest on the wires. There are many seagulls.
My trousers grow used to the dung.
What news from the frontier? Is Donald still Colonel?
Are there more pupils than teachers in Scotland?
I send you this by a small boy with a pointed head.
Don't trust him. He is a Campbell.

(2)

The dog brought your letter today
from the red postbox on the stone gate
two miles away and a bit.
I read it carefully with tears in my eyes.
At night the moon is high over Cladach
and the big mansions of prosperous Englishmen.
I drank a half bottle thinking of Meg
and the involved affairs of Scotland.
When shall we two meet again
in thunder, lightning or in rain?
The carrots and turnips are healthy,
the *Farmers' Weekly* garrulous.
Please send me a *Radio Times* and a book
on cracking codes. I have much sorrow.
Mrs Macleod has a blue lion on her pants.
They make a queenly swish in a high wind.

(3)

There is a man here who has been building a house
for twenty years and a day.
He has a barrow in which he carries large stones.
He wears a canvas jacket.

205

I think I am going out of my mind.
When shall I see the city again,
its high towers and insurance offices,
its glare of unprincipled glass?
The hens peck at the grain.
The wind brings me pictures of exiles,
ghosts in tackety boots, lies,
adulteries in cornfields and draughty cottages.
I hear Donald is a brigadier now
and that there is fighting on the frontier.
The newspapers arrive late with strange signs on them.
I go out and watch the road.

(4)

Today I read five books.
I watched Macleod weaving a fence
to keep the eagles from his potatoes.
A dull horse is cobwebbed in rain.
When shall our land consider itself safe
from the assurance of the third rate mind?
We lack I think nervous intelligence.
Tell them I shall serve in any capacity,
a field officer, even a private,
so long as I can see the future
through uncracked field glasses.

(5)

A woman arrived today
in a brown coat and a brown muff.
She says we are losing the war,
that the Emperor's troops are everywhere
in their blue armour and blue gloves.
She says there are men in a stupor
in the ditches among the marigolds
crying 'Alas, alas.'
I refuse to believe her.
She is, I think, an agent provocateur.
She pretends to breed thistles.

from THE NOTEBOOKS OF ROBINSON CRUSOE

(11)

The wind blows in my chimney. How mournful it is! I can hear in it voices of exhortation, of warning, and of regret.
They speak of partings, wrecks and exile. They remind of crimes inflicted on others and on oneself.
O that I were a man without memory, a machine renewed by the days, a tree that forgets its autumn leaves, its winter dispossessions.
O that like a cock I could crow in the morning, my red hackles duplicating the sun's rays, my head fierce and singular, my brassy extended throat dispersing the rack of clouds.

(12)

Last night I drank much rum. I dreamed that you were in my arms. Later I talked without ceasing.
Waking from my dishevelled bed, I entered a world so tidy that I wept as you wept. If I had my mother's clock, with the two Dutch figures, I would stay in the dark to watch you step out in your green sabots.
But you are not there, the climate is constant, and the only speaker is Pretty Poll who speaks beady eyed and without humour the words, 'Crusoe . . . Cruise . . . Crew,' from the world of his squalor, riffling his feathers, regarding me from his red cage as I walk by the ruffled sea.

(14)

LANDSCAPE

This landscape is my diary.
I inscribe the day on it.
I invest it with grammar.
The rack of rocks I compose
in the blowing wind.
I say, 'That apple tree
reminds me of someone.
I hang my ghosts on it,
hairily entering the sea.'

(17)

In my leafed chapel I pray to God.
I say to myself: I am better than spastics, idiots, physically ruined men.
I do not have TB, cancer, heart disease, or any plague.
My heart, lungs, kidneys, liver are sound.
I do not suffer the tremors of the bank clerk or the tempests of the manager.
I do not pace up and down in a hospital waiting for the doctor to tell me about my wife and whether the haemorrhages have stopped.
I do not hear the crazy white-haired violinist scraping in the attic.
I am not feverish with love.
I do not phone my sweetheart at midnight from a squalid bar, nor do I see her raising her shadowy lips to her lover's, behind a closed curtain.
I do not stand by a stretcher watching the pale mouth hardly breathing.
I do not see my children returning from the arena beaten.
I do not stand before the blank wall of my disabilities.
For all these things I give thanks to God.
Why then am I not happy?

(19)

Last night I saw in the moonlight standing by a tree Jim Merrick whose last biscuit I ate on a raft in the Indian Ocean just before he died. His bearded face vibrated like the rings of the tree and then changed into seaweed pulsating with miniature fish.

I stayed by my hut, my bones rattling like dice in a cup, my sleepless lidless eyes steadily dilating.

Later by the candle, my breast heated by rum, I heard a bell ring distinct and near.

How much of the Bible I read I cannot remember nor how many souls betrayed, insatiable, writhed on the capsizing walls till dawn.

(21)

March and the world is white again
like notepaper, like a newspaper.
I could write a letter
of the plainest marble.
The wind goes over and over.
I am a fictional character
in the white newspaper.
Someone on a liner
is reading me.

(24)

I shall clamp my teeth.
I shall not bleed language.
If my condition is absurd let it be so.

Let me be steel. Irony's not enough.
I shall go down into my grave
below these foreign blooms.

Starlight dangles towards me. Let me wave
my handkerchief to the universe.
This is no place for rage.

I am the parrot of a lost routine.
I have a splendid cage
central to this green.

This is a comic place.
I shall carve my name on the trees
over and over.

It is possible that I shall grow used to this as a knot to wood and that, were rescuers brisk with pity and self congratulation, to emerge from the sea I should hide in the woods and like an animal peer at them fearfully between the slats of leaves.

It is possible that, aware of my kingship here, I would not return to anonymity there but that, breeding hauteur in my solitude, I should recoil from the momentary and dramatic solicitude of others.

For the oyster in the depths of the sea has its pearl as I my arrogance and, constant to my own sufficiency, I would disdain the million wandering fish sliding past, each on his own level.

It is possible that, my own god worshipping my own images, I would not wish to enter, unshaven and hairy, the monotonous climate of the mediocre, but would prefer my extreme pain to their temperate ordinariness.

O Lord, let me know my mortality: let me cast myself on the common waters. Let me be resurrected by the cheap tarnished glorious tinfoil light.

(28)

NAMES

I

Noon: and the gluttonous ocean sparkles. I know that it can drown me, that its fish can fine me down to bone. I know the capabilities of its factory.
Nevertheless how can I nail my 'sea' to sea, my 'hill' to hill. And how can my 'well' furnish me with water?

II

And how can my 'ought' emerge from this summer? From its multiplicity of leaves, its unknown flowers, its whirr of ignorant insects.
How can the data erect a ladder? How can the immigrant lay down his rules?
How can the green shade breed its commandments? Or the snake, with its typical hissing, sway its small head against mine?

III

I walk about, egotist of the day, yet the beast bird and insect have their own concerns, are enveloped in their own armour. My

philosophy is the excess of leisure, my religion the questionings of idleness.
Yet to exist is to be vain: to move is to be noticed.
The snake rears itself like a question, interrogating eternity.

(30)

Island, what shall I say of you, your peat bogs, your lochs, your moors and berries?
The cry of your birds in the fading evening.
Your flowers in summer glowing brightly where there are no thoroughfares.
The perpetual sound of the sea.
The spongy moss on which feet imprint themselves.
The mountains which darken and brighten like ideas in the mind.
The owl with its big glasses that perches on a late tree listening.
The mussels clamped to the rocks, the fool's gold, the tidal pools filling and emptying.
The corn that turns from pale green to yellow, my scarecrow rattling in the wind.
The smoke that arises from my fire.

This I say:
One man cannot warm the world.
This I say:
The world of one man is different from the world of many men.

This I say:
Without the net, the sweetest fish are tasteless.

(33)

When they rescue me I shall return to the perfumed vaudevilles and machinery, to the music halls of the fat sopranos, to the Master of Ceremonies with the tucked tails, the moustache, the stick and the voluminous words. I shall see the advertisements which illuminate the sky, our homes of Viyella, Vibroso and Vitamins.
I shall leave my bare island, simple as poison, to enter the equally poisonous world of Tiberius, where there are echoes and reflections, a Hall of Mirrors in which my face like all faces swells like a jester's in a world without sense.

211

I have read them all, Sartre, Wittgenstein, Ryle. I have listened at midday to the actresses popstars authors in "Desert Island Discs" speculating happily on islands among the traffic of London (Am I allowed dettol and bandages? Voltaire?)

And as I remember hell, the choice of staying by the communal inferno where we feed on each other or going alone into the middle of the dark wood leaving behind me forever the Pickwicks and the iced candles of Christmas, I hear now clearly in the hollow spaces of the valleys, in the roar of the waterfall, in the appearance of the birds of spring and their departure in the autumn the same phrase repeated over and over:

Language is other people.

It is not with sorrow that I stand on deck and leave behind me the island and the thirty years of my life there.

It is rather with puzzlement as if a dream were beginning again, the dream of officers in white, seamen in blue, television cameras, the manic unblinking eye of the announcer. The enigma of the dream persists as the jovial captain at the head of yards of white linen quizzes me, between draughts of wine: as the sailors weave about me their human erotic legends!

As the ship steadily steers towards the cameras providing rich merchandise for my new dream and I emerge from the world of sparse iron into the vast cinema of sensation.

X

IN SLEEP

Sometimes when I sleep I am among the dead.
They are all laughing and joking.
They walk along the road just like live people,
and their clothes are not at all old-fashioned.
When I wake up we drive through the early morning mist
past lochs which are as calm as plates.
The sun has not yet risen and the world is quiet.
The roses hang their heads among the dew.

WHEN DAY IS DONE

Sorrow remembers us when day is done.
It sits in its old chair gently rocking
and singing tenderly in the evening.
It welcomes us home again after the day.
It is so old in its black silken dress,
its stick beside it carved with legends.
It tells its stories over and over again.
After a while we have to stop listening.

THE COOL WEATHER

After the tropical heat was over
it came down to grey weather once again,
and we welcomed it. We liked the grey weather.
We were more used to that than to the heat
or the colourful emporium of the tropics.
After all our art is more like that
than it is like Gauguin for example.
Then there was Cromwell and morality.
Deep inside us we like grey weather
the cool days so pure and unemphatic.
What loud statements could we now make
what towering birds glowering in the thicket?

215

IN YELLOW

The Chinamen sing Chinese songs
as they go round the bamboo tree
and their faces are all yellow
and the tunes of their songs are very strange

and the canary settles on the washing line
and sings all morning
its sweet canary song —
while the shapeless clothes are drying.
It is a fine day for everyone,
for canaries and for Chinamen
and for the clothes slowly gaining their shape.

MORNING

The white egg boils in the new saucepan
The toaster flips another toast upwards.
The window is open on the drenched field
where the calf is loose again among the haystacks.

Our jobs await us but the radio says
'Love is everything.' The disc jockey
is brushed and frivolous beside the mike
speaking of streets and towns he hasn't seen.

The road points the house towards the office.
The hens are laying eggs. Someone bakes bread.
We hammer the calf's stake into the ground
Around the iron fades the fresh dew.

IN OTHER PLACES

In other places all sorts of things are going on,
the emaciated beggars won't eat mutton.
The rickshaws and sampans colour the East,
soldiers with wooden legs go home to rest.

These things are at the corner of your mind
grazing vaguely like cows in a meadow.

Eventually you add up the columns once again.
Sighing heavily, you add up the columns.

PUPIL'S HOLIDAY JOB

The girl who was reading Milton
is at the cash desk in the supermarket.
Her glasses are too large for her pale face.
The bread and milk slide down the same slope
followed by the meat and oranges.
It is possible that there are many worlds—
Lycidas, where are you Lycidas?
You are locked in a school of old paint
you die inside a grille of pale windows.
The bill comes to pounds and pounds and pounds.
A whole week's groceries in front of you
and your pale face has glasses large and round.
Lycidas is floating in the sea
among bouquets and the eternal monsters
with strange names, so Greek, so salt with brine.
Down the slope the bread and cereals pour,
they pour eternally with Lycidas.
He's turning over and over with the cartons
in the sea of everyday with all its monsters.

THE THEATRE

The theatre that we found among the trees
is putting on a new season of plays.
Strindberg rages among foliage
and Ibsen hasn't reached his final autumn.

The plays go on and on as the leaves change.
In that bright box our feelings coruscate.
Below the stage what words have changed to coal—
what skulls look upward with their black mouths?

IF EVER YOU LOVED ME

If ever you loved me
tell me about the misty medals,
the brooches with fog on them,
and the graveyards that do not blossom.

If ever you loved me
do not send me mint-scented envelopes
or telegrams telling me to visit
your brisk abysses.

THE TORCHES

The newspapers create news.
The poets create poems.
Everyone illuminates his acre
with a hugged torch.

And the skeletons clash in the wind
like a wash of old clothes.
The horizon chases its tail
over and over.

THIS BUBBLE

In this stained bubble
we live together
all of us

taking up telescopes now and again
to watch the Far Country
where the sounds of dancing come from

the inebriated voices
wholly abandoned to the moment
the people who wear the wild skins
we have long cast off.

THE CHAIR

The tall green-backed chair
in a room with brown walls
and all the old questions
start here.

If I had met you elsewhere
if you had dried your tears
with a different handkerchief
in a different hand—

and the tall green-backed chair
seems so fixed and solid
like a family lawyer
in all the thunderstorms.

MY CHILD

My child, where are you?
The woods are waning
and I am seeking you among the hedges.

I am still wearing my stiff gown
which often sustained you
among the stones and thistles.

I bring you the right shape of things.
I bring you the warm bread
with the crust on it.

I bring you the bottles
with the white milk in them,
the knives and the spoons.

I bring you our house with the rigid roof on it,
the cupboards with their groceries,
the wardrobes with your ironed clothes.

I bring you the made bed,
the fire with the red voice,
the rectangular windows.

Child, I am looking for you.

They tell me you are in the rivers
growing haphazardly
dabbled in water.

My voice comes to you across the cornstacks,
across my completed harvest,
across the sharp stubble.

WOMEN

Bewildered and angry is the sap of women
as if the tree were to fight against itself
in a hurt greenness, in a swaying current,
in a wrestle to put out flowers or thorns.

Man often strolls down an avenue of ideas,
his hands in his pockets cool and lenient.
It is the morning for a cigarette
or for a joke from his worn pack of cards.

Woman sees no humour in the sky.
Earth is a purse which feeds us.
The tidied child is heading towards marriage
and then a fixed place in the earth,

or perhaps in astrology, that favoured village,
which sheds names sensibly and certainly.
The girl walks in the steps of Pisces,
in the chains of Virgo, in its green lanes.

Man measures the stars' heat and incidence,
their probability, their constituents.
Their naval and other councils are formal.
Their disentangled language is of weather.

Women follow the moon down yellow pages,
their bodies shaken by winds, teeth chattering.
Their roots whine and sing. They grip their acre.
Sometimes they float out on eerie tides.

TEARS ARE SALT

Tears are salt like the sea.
How reality breaks in on us
while we are acting so well
on our tiny stages,

dressed up so sunnily
wearing our brooches and belts
considering the world
as just about our size.

Suddenly reality is there
with its large crude torch
shining it into our eyes
and into our guts.

The sunbeam just passing
is carrying a coffin
as a bee will carry pollen
home to its hive.

In the centre of the tear
is a small inverted man
gazing down at the sky
and a pair of dusty shoes.

Tears are salt like the sea.
Standing together
we look out from the headland
at a mouth burbling with foam.

IN THE MIDDLE

In the middle
flashings,
shakings and glitterings.

Arms that come from the right,
arms that come from the left.

Whispers at corners. 'Is Hamlet better? Is Sarah?
Where are the flowers of spring, ah, where are they?'

Notes that are sent about thunder,
cards about lightning,
chairs that tower like skeletons out of the storm.

Is he well? Is he ill? Bring me my burning chariot,
my helmet, my sceptre, my mail of the yellowest gold.

Arms that come from the right,
papers that come from the left,
posts that breathlessly rush over moorland and road.

What is on fire? Is it my heart? Is it Scotland?
Who is that fellow? Have him put in the stocks
till his hair is singed and his body burns like a crab.

Where is the note I left on top of that tomb?

Someone is painting the walls in a downpour of purple.

Glintings,
shakings,
and flashings.

A postbag of clouds.

NONE IS THE SAME AS ANOTHER

None is the same as another,
O none is the same.

That none is the same as another
is matter for crying
since never again will you see
that one, once gone.

In their brown hoods
the pilgrims are crossing the land
and many will look the same
but all are different

and their ideas fly to them
on accidental winds
perching awhile in their minds
from different valleys.

None is the same as another,
O none is the same.

And that none is the same is not
a matter for crying.

Stranger, I take your hand,
O changing stranger.

THE IOLAIRE

The green washed over them. I saw them when
the New Year brought them home. It was a day
that orbed the horizon with an enigma.
It seemed that there were masts. It seemed that men
buzzed in the water round them. It seemed that fire
shone in the water which was thin and white
unravelling towards the shore. It seemed that I
touched my fixed hat which seemed to float and then
the sun illumined fish and naval caps,
names of the vanished ships. In sloppy waves,
in the fat of water, they came floating home
bruising against their island. It is true
a minor error can inflict this death,
that star is not responsible. It shone
over the puffy blouse, the flapping blue
trousers, the black boots. The seagulls swam
bonded to the water. Why not man?
The lights were lit last night, the tables creaked
with hoarded food. They willed the ship to port
in the New Year which would erase the old,
its errant voices, its unpractised tones.
Have we done ill, I ask? My sober hat
floated in the water, my fixed body
a simulacrum of the transient waste,
for everything was mobile, planks that swayed,
the keeling ship exploding, and the splayed
cold insect bodies. I have seen your church
solid. This is not. The water pours
into the parting timbers where I ache
above the globular eyes. The slack heads turn
ringing the horizon without a sound
with mortal bells, a strange exuberant flower
unknown to our dry churchyards. I look up.
The sky begins to brighten as before,
remorseless amber, and the bruised blue grows
at the erupting edges. I have known you, God,
not as the playful one but as the black
thunderer from hills. I kneel
and touch this dumb blonde head. My hand is scorched.
Its human quality confuses me.
I have not felt such hair so dear before

nor seen such real eyes. I kneel from you.
This water soaks me. I am running with
its tart sharp joy. I am floating here.
In my black uniform, I am embraced
by these green ignorant waters. I am calm.

ON AN ICY DAY

We walk on mirrors today just like Hamlet.
The state is as slippery as this, and just as subtle.
What contortions we must make to keep our balance!

With rosettes on our shoes we almost dance as we go.
What is the yellow bird perched on glass, is it Osric
in his folds of transparent gullery, extravagantly winged?

And what is that face in the mirror? Is it Claudius
blowing his drunken trumpet, power at the source?

The ordinary folk are sliding hither and thither.
They never look in the mirror but straight ahead of them
towards the shrunken branches, baskets clutched in their hands.

SPEECH FOR PROSPERO

When I left that island I thought I was dead. Nothing
stirred in me. Miranda in jeans
and totally innocent was standing by a sail
and all the others, happily recovered, talking
in suits made of brine. But to return to

the gossip, the poisonous ring, was not easy,
and many times I nearly tried to turn back
feeling in my bones the desolate hum of the headland,
my creation of rivers and mist.

Still we went on. The corruptible had put on flesh,
the young were hopeful once again, all was forgiven.
Nevertheless the waiters were scraping and bowing,
the rumours beginning, the crowns of pure crystal were sparkling,
the telephones were ringing with messages from the grave
and the thin phosphorescent boys glowing with ambition
in corners of velvet and death.

Still I went on. The ship left its wake behind it
shining and fading, cord of a new birth,
and over by the sail Miranda gazed at her prince
yearning for love.

Goodbye, island, never again shall I see you,
you are part of my past. Though I may dream of you often
I know there's a future we all must learn to accept
music working itself out in the absurd halls and the mirrors
posturings of men like birds, Art in a torrent of plates,
the sound of the North wind distant yet close
as stairs ascend from the sea.

CHINESE POEM

The darkness lightens. The yellow army sets out
on horseback past the waterfall.
The grizzled general searches the clouds.
Back in her kitchen the tearful girl is scrubbing
but the Great Wall must be defended
from the barbarians.
If he should not come back . . . It is always the same.
The widow sits in a grey house
gently stroking the hair that is buried
among the rushes.

The charge, the charge! He has forgotten her
when the dust rises, hiding the helmets,
and the Emperor issues his orders from a thundercloud.
The Great Wall must not break.
Honour is not a word written on parchment
nor is it like a duck that flies into the sunset
negligently.

Honour is what keeps the mulberry bush fresh
the woman safe at her baking
the courageous general upright on his horse.

He will not come back till the spring perhaps
and even then
he may be bent and limping under the weight of his glory.
His eyes may be touched by barbarism.
Still she will bow to him as before
like the grass in front of the wind.

THE RED HORSE

'Art costs everything,' I said.
'Think of the red
horse in the field
abandoned by everyone but itself.

Even the generals leave the dead
bones shimmering quietly in the heat
and would love to ride
the magnificent red steed.

So, she is weeping quietly at the sink
submissive as a horse that has been tamed.
The plum tree in the garden points north,
to where the lean priest in yellow weather
studies the waterfall.

The clouds move towards him. He rides away
on his red horse towards a sound of battle.
Grey is her hair, obedient like the rushes.
No messenger comes ever to her door.
The sound of war is distant.'

AUTUMN

Autumn again. A wide-eyed absence in
the woods and skies. The trees, once berry-ripe,
are cleared of weight and in the midday shine

forlorn, perhaps. Triumphant. It is true
that exile, parting, is our earthly lot
though roots cling tight below the green and blue.
O handkerchiefs wave free while the full heart
is squeezed of purple leaving the wrinkled skin.
Depend on everything depend on art,
your crystal table set with paper, pen,
such simple instruments. Begin once more.
Spring in its fury breaks on us again
frizzle of summer, winter with its snow,
and also autumn — beating the hazels down
from trees enriched by taste and by red hue.

Art feeds us, famished. It's the heavenly crown,
the earthly crown against the distant blue.

RUNNING REPAIRS

A fight? she asks. A button from your blazer
torn by a boy? Well, I'll replace it now.
She sights the black thread through an invisible needle,
then tugs the button tight. Stay there. O how
can the whole world be perfect as a button?
Lost for a moment she remembers some
earlier button that she would sew on.
But there's an end of it, his mouth is dumb.
Buttons and thread, our life is all repairs
and sudden quarrels. Unbuttoned in his tomb
no longer open to the fighting airs
he stepped to death out of the living room.
There, that's finished. Mind it's tight enough.
In his black blazer he carelessly turns away.
The thread is dangling elsewhere, long as love.
The needle pierces, almost subsumed by day.

SPEECH FOR A WOMAN

One night
I saw my children
climbing the stairs in the frost
which had carved an unintelligible language
on the single window.

'Where have you been?' I asked
for they were whistling
and talking about the magic games they had played
in green ferocious shirts.

'Everywhere,' they said.
'especially where the blue sky blackens
under the weight of the future:
and particularly in a desert in which we saw
a woman in a brown shawl waving.
Ships we took, trains we took, and the green buses
that flowed across a country under siege,
where the same woman with an empty mouth
spoke of eternal famine.'

The whistling faded,
I opened the door of their room.
It was tidier than I had ever seen it.
The sweaty socks were not to be seen
nor the embroidered jerseys
nor the records with the satanic drums
nor the pictures.

It was a sacred shrine that I was looking at.
Slowly the clock began to tick
and it flowed through my whole body
which was a dress of sand
emptying like an hourglass as I gazed.

MY BROTHER

My brother, today the rain is falling,
I haven't heard from you for twenty years.
When you left first you were so confident,
riding your new horse from coast to coast.
Then after a while you stopped writing.
My letters never reached you for you changed addresses.
Were you ashamed that your new horse never lasted?
Sailors from the old country have seen you in bars
but you don't speak to them.
Success is demanded of the exile.
Today as the rain falls it occurred to me
that I do not know where you are.
How the world comes between even two brothers!
All I can see is the horse you wrote of
standing in a cage of rain somewhere
with the burrs of twenty years on its skin.

I REMEMBER I REMEMBER

I remember I remember the house where I was born,
there were roses made of light and a laburnum tree.

It must have been in a different country, black lady,
who sit in the chair rocking and stare at me.

I swung through the blue air towards you,
merciless Muse, with the black watch on your wrist.

The air, the air . . . Throw the big windows wide.
The boy is playing his violin among the stones.

REMEMBERING

When the wind blows the curtains wide, do you not remember
the green trams on their wires and yourself young,
singing on a street that no one now can find.
It is as if the book opens, showing the parts you have played
in a theatre more precious to you than The Globe
with its ghostly flags flying in an Elizabethan wind.

OLD WOMAN

Your face is wrinkled
with the roads you have travelled
The vows you have made
to the crockery
Your beauty
shines through old age
like an old boat in a strait
fishing in the blaze
of a last sunset.